PELICAN BOOKS

A513

GOD IN ACTION

F. A. COCKIN

F. A. COCKIN

GOD IN ACTION

*A STUDY IN THE
HOLY SPIRIT*

PENGUIN BOOKS

Penguin Books Ltd, Harmondsworth, Middlesex
U.S.A.: Penguin Books Inc., 3300 Clipper Mill Road, Baltimore 11, Md
AUSTRALIA: Penguin Books Pty Ltd, 762 Whitehorse Road,
Mitcham, Victoria

—

First published 1961

—

Made and printed in Great Britain
by R. & R. Clark Ltd
Edinburgh

To my Wife

CONTENTS

INTRODUCTION

THE original invitation to write this book was somewhat oddly phrased. It was suggested that what was needed was 'a non-theological book on the Holy Spirit'.

It would be difficult to think of a more superb contradiction in terms. And yet one knew perfectly well what the author of the remark had in mind. And one knew also that he was right.

Anyone in the least sensitive to the climate of contemporary thought knows what is implied by 'non-theological'. At the simplest level there is the plea for the avoidance as far as possible of technical language, or at least for the introduction of the great classical words of Christian doctrine only after an attempt has been made to give them an intelligible context, the picture for instance of a human situation in which it would be natural to speak of 'redeeming' an apparently hopeless position.

More serious than that of course is the implication that to call a book 'theological' is to warn off at sight some of those whom one might most want to read it. For to many of them, men and women of intelligence and moral seriousness, theology appears quite irrelevant to the intellectual and ethical perplexities of which they are conscious, if not a perverse attempt to find a solution in terms which they have ceased to regard as having any validity.

I have made such attempt as I can to pay due regard to these conditions. In the two opening chapters I have tried at least to indicate an awareness of the doubts and perplexities which beset many minds in their whole approach to religion: and to make plain how much leeway I believe the Church has to make up, both in thought and in action, before it is likely to regain a respectful hearing for the Christian view. The same point is taken up again in Chapters 8–10.

But there is a further difficulty. It has become a common-place to say that the doctrine of the Holy Spirit is the least understood and most disregarded of the central beliefs of Christianity. And the statement is no more than the truth. There is a lamentable dearth of first-class literature on the subject, compared to the quantity available on, for instance, the doctrines of the Incarnation or the Atonement. And it is safe to infer that this means a comparable neglect in the teaching given, whether in theological colleges or in preaching. To a considerable extent one is writing in a vacuum.

The only way of meeting this seemed to be to devote a considerable section of the book (Chapters 3–6) to an attempt to bring out as vividly as possible the extraordinary contrast between this state of inattention and ignorance and the position revealed by a study of the New Testament as the record of the original Christian experience.

And here I had better make a frank confession. Twenty years ago I wrote a small book, *The Holy Spirit and the Church*, in which I devoted a good deal of space to a similar review of the evidence. That book has been out of print and unobtainable for a number of years. And it therefore seemed permissible to use some of that material again, though it has been almost entirely rewritten.

The life of a diocesan bishop does not leave a great deal of time for keeping abreast of the progress of Biblical scholarship. I cannot make any claim to be familiar with the latest view on the authenticity of some of the 'Pauline' Epistles, or on the compilation of the Book of Acts. I have quite frankly taken much of the evidence as it stands, as presenting an over-all picture of the experience and beliefs of the first-century Church, without for instance seeking to draw a very sharp distinction between Pauline and Johannine strands of thought. What I hope does emerge from this presentation is the unquestionable fact that in this formative period the reality of a directing and controlling force which they call 'the

Spirit' is absolutely central. If that is so, it must inevitably follow that a failure, or at any rate only a very intermittent attempt, to explore and respond to that influence throughout the history of the Church will have had the most serious effects both upon our progressive understanding of our faith and upon our moral and spiritual vitality in facing the demands of ever-changing human situations.

The earlier book made little attempt to carry the inquiry beyond the end of the period covered by the New Testament evidence. In this book I have undertaken a rather more ambitious task. Clearly, if one is seeking to discover indications of the Spirit of God at work, whether inside or outside the life of the Church today, one must attempt at least to discern the signs of his influence throughout the centuries of Christian history. Here quite frankly I realize that I have attempted something which is beyond my powers – and indeed, I would think, most men's. To suggest that in a chapter or two one can even collect some of the clues which may guide us in such a work of detection is almost effrontery. I can only hope that it has not been done in such a way as might misrepresent the truth.

The concluding chapters return again to the theme of the two opening ones. I have taken up some of the major demands with which, as I see it, the Church is confronted in our time: the need to vindicate the truth of the Christian view of human life in face of widespread scepticism; the need to demonstrate the relevance of Christian faith to urgent human needs, political, economic, and social; the need to remove the crying scandal of disunion; the need to demonstrate the reality of Christian discipleship. And I have tried to indicate in each of these spheres the distinctive gift for which, if the New Testament is a true guide, we should look to the Spirit.

I said that the existing literature was scanty. But I have drawn freely on such sources as I know. I hope that due acknowledgement of these has been made either in the text or in the short Bibliography.

Finally let me acknowledge a debt of gratitude to three friends, Dr Kathleen Bliss, the Rev. Eric Fenn, and the Dean of Bristol, who have given most liberally of advice and criticism at more than one stage of the writing, and to my wife, who, at a moment when she might fairly have expected to enjoy the fruits of retirement, bought a new typewriter and resumed her occupation of many years ago as my secretary.

CHAPTER I

The Religious Predicament

AT the core of our beliefs, I suppose, lies the conviction that the age of religion is past. Once upon a time it had a central part to play both in our picture of nature, and in our moral and social ideas. But men's ideas about nature have developed to a point at which, like Laplace, they no longer have any need to bring in religious concepts and hypotheses: and religion no longer dictates to us our ideas about morality and society – with the result that neither scientifically nor politically does it any longer 'fit in'. This has come about not as a result of any formal disproof of the chief religious claims: theology is not a formal, mathematical subject like geometry, in which knock-down arguments can be looked for. Rather, it has lost its place cumulatively, as the result of a long series of retreats and withdrawals: and, without feeling its necessity on our own pulses, we can hardly be expected to create a place for it afresh.

I ought to say something too about morals and religion. My parents, I believe, broke with the religious bodies in which they had been brought up because they valued their moral convictions so deeply. ... How often, looking back at history, does one find religion serving as an instrument not only of social conformity but of communal rivalry.

That is one reason why I, and my like, hope – as well as believe – that the age of religion is past.

Well, there we have it, plain and unvarnished; the outspoken statement, on the air, of a deliberate, dispassionate conviction that religion is, or should be, a thing of the past, and of a hope that it is. And if anyone objects that that is only the kind of thing you would expect from high-brows on the Third Programme (on which indeed Professor Toulmin's talk was given), the answer is only too easy. The workers on the floor of the rolling mills in Sheffield, or an aircraft factory in Bristol, do not indeed express themselves with the same elegance or restraint as a University lecturer. But their views on this subject are at least as emphatic.

It is worth spending a moment (though we shall have to return to this point later on at greater length) to note the two counts on which religion is here dismissed. Speculatively, it finds no place in the investigation and description of the ever-expanding universe which the natural sciences reveal to us. Practically, it has ceased to exercise any serious or valuable influence on the solution of problems of conduct or the ordering of human society.

That this total dismissal of religion as an outworn relic is widespread needs no demonstration. It is the sincere conviction of men and women of ability and integrity, who are as concerned as any believer with the perplexities and problems of our time. It is equally the avowed aim and policy of those who seek to dominate the world in the interests of Marxist ideology.

But it is by no means characteristic of all those who find themselves unable to accept the traditional forms of Christian belief and worship. There are others who do not share Professor Toulmin's satisfaction in the disappearance of religious faith, or his hope that it will never again exercise an effective influence in human life. Another quotation, this time from a broadcast talk by Mr J. P. Corbett, brings out a very different attitude.

Our society has long been divided between those who are comfortably settled within the bosom of a Church, and those who are hostile or indifferent to every vestige of religion. Across this chasm nothing seems to pass. The doubts, the criticisms, the denials of the one side, and the appeals, the assertions, the reassurances of the other, fall to the ground like so many paper darts, and are trampled underfoot amongst the business of the world.

If neither the atheists nor the believers – to judge by the faintness of their words – can make themselves heard across this chasm, then it is left to us agnostics, to us who feel something of the pull, and see something of the sense, of either side, to do what we can to make communication possible between them.

If we are to be true to our programme as agnostics we must seek out the true substance of religious experience and religious thought, the true substance whose dim but powerful presence to our minds makes it impossible for us to turn our backs upon the world of faith, the true substance which has been dressed out, to meet the needs of earlier societies, in forms which are intolerable to our own.

The speaker went on to give a moving statement of personal experience: of the suffering which springs continually from unsatisfied desire; of the striving to which that suffering stirs us; of the growing realization that nothing within the confines of human achievement, scientific knowledge, invention, social amelioration, can ever bring the satisfaction we seek.

We set out from a kind of suffering, and continue with a kind of effort which, though they arise from ordinary experience, are yet utterly unlike anything else that it contains: and we end with a power beyond ourselves, whose existence, whose greatness, and whose goodness are as impossible to describe and establish as they are necessary to accept.

And he ended:

We discover by hard experience that the more we try to make ourselves absolute master of our lives, the less life there is left to master. We are prepared to recognize this mystery rather than to overlook it: to depend upon it rather than upon our own bravado, and to accept whatever words and practices may make it possible for us to utter our conviction that we are bound equally to one another in a perfection which transcends us all, whether the forms of faith are old or new, lasting or fugitive, Christian or non-Christian, ecclesiastical or lay.

I make no apology for quoting at length from these two talks, because they present us at first-hand with two typical expressions of the contemporary mood. On the one hand a flat rejection of the whole religious past of humanity. We have done with that. We turn elsewhere for the answer to our questions, and the satisfaction of our needs. And on the other the expression of a deep distress and concern, which spring on the one hand from the realization that the traditional formulations, the theologies, the liturgies, even the matchless parables, have lost their compelling power; and on the other from a certainty, born of experience of life itself, that without the ultimate truth which they once conveyed and still symbolize no lasting satisfaction is to be found.

If, as I believe, these two attitudes reflect the situation and the outlook of very many men and women at the present time – including of course plenty who could never express their feelings in these articulate forms – then inevitably we are faced with the question: How has this come to be? It is not enough – indeed it is a grave betrayal of Christian responsibility – merely to write off these attitudes as 'hostile', 'sceptical', and 'indifferent', and to leave it at that. Why do all these people feel as they do? Whose fault is it that traditional faith and worship no longer register? That is the question which must be answered.

The answer is in one sense a commonplace. But it is a commonplace which, when examined in depth, is seen to raise issues of a range and complexity which it would take us far beyond the limits of an introductory chapter to explore.

Within our lifetime we have witnessed, not indeed the full flowering – for that still lies ahead – but an immensely rapid maturing, of the Scientific Revolution. Its roots of course run back into the seventeenth century. But within the last hundred, and with ever increasing momentum within the last fifty, years its full impact has made itself felt, transforming man's outlook not only upon the nature of the universe, but upon his own standing and significance within it.

It may well seem ludicrously presumptuous to attempt within a few pages even to illustrate its nature and effects. But perhaps a thumb-nail sketch may serve to set our imagination at work, and thereby lead us to a more realistic appreciation of some of the forces which are shaping the experience and the thinking of our generation.

Of the verdict passed by those competent to judge on the scale and significance of scientific advance there can be no doubt. Here are a couple of well-known quotations, the one from a historian, the other from a scientist.

The first is from Professor Butterfield.*

The scientific revolution outshines everything since the rise of Christianity, and reduces the Renaissance and the Reformation to mere episodes, mere internal displacements within mediaeval Christendom. ... The seventeenth century indeed did not merely bring a new factor into history – one that must just be added, so to speak, to the other permanent factors. The new factor [like a cuckoo in a hedge-sparrow's nest, if one may insert a simile of one's own] began immediately to elbow out the other ones, and indeed began immediately to seek control of the rest. The result has been the emergence of a kind of civilization which could cut itself away from its Graeco-Roman heritage, away from Christianity itself – only too confident in its power to exist independent of anything of the kind.

The second is from Sir Lawrence Bragg.†

How does the advance of science rate as an event in the history of mankind? I accept the view that it is one of the major events which at long intervals quite transform the whole nature of human life. The discovery of the scientific method, and the vastly increased power to penetrate the secrets of nature and to control its forces, which has arisen directly or indirectly from the advance of science, constitute an event comparable in importance to the change from a hunting or pastoral to an agricultural way of life. ... What we are witnessing is the start of a new era, a mysterious unknown x, which will bear in importance the same relation to civilization that civilization bears to barbarism.

* H. Butterfield, *Origins of Modern Science* (Bell, 1949), pp. viii, 174.
† Radford Mather Lecture, quoted in Oldham, *Life is Commitment* (S.C.M., 1953), to which, for much of this section, I am greatly indebted.

We can discern three main directions in which this revolution has produced unmistakable effects.

There is the immense expansion of knowledge; and even more significant, the fact that this expansion has come through the use and refinement of a particular method of research, experimentation, and verification, the success of which has given it enormous prestige. Second there is the development of man's sense of power. The late Mr Michael Foster noted a significant shift of emphasis, in the scientific outlooks of the ancient and of the modern world, which he described by the contrast between 'mystery' and 'mastery'. Greek science was in essence contemplative, 'the conforming of the mind to nature', the attempt to enter into and comprehend the secrets of a natural environment, which, as interpreted by the Christian mind, itself reflected a divine order. The change came when Descartes spoke of 'a new Physics which will make men lords and possessors of nature'. And the growth of technology in the last century is sufficient commentary on that text.

But the most significant effect, arising almost unconsciously out of the use of this knowledge and power, is the change in man's estimate of his own status in relation to his world. The limits of man's capacity to take his destiny into his own hands are being steadily pushed further back. Knowledge, it was said at the beginning of the scientific revolution, is power. It has now become something more. Knowledge is salvation.

It is worth while spending a moment or two reflecting a little further on these three characteristics. Even a very amateur acquaintance with the principles and methods of scientific inquiry reveals a number of points at which preoccupation with it can be seen to have very definite effects upon men's attitude to the characteristic methods and sanctions of the religious approach to reality.

There is first the deliberate selection of a carefully defined field of inquiry, and the choice of instruments and techniques appropriate to that particular undertaking. The nature of the inquiry is such that the results can normally be checked and counterchecked by the repetition of the experiment. The characteristic notes are precision, controllability, verification. It does not take much imagination to realize how alien is the world into which the scientist feels that he is entering when he encounters the typical presentation of religious, even in some measure theological, truth. A brilliant young physicist of my acquaintance, who went to one of the ancient universities to read theology, remarked at the end of his first term: 'This is a very puzzling business. I've spent the whole of my time so far trying to discover a *fact*!'

There is the severe disciplining and control of the personal equation. It is of course nonsense to suppose that the scientist works without the impulse of strong emotional drives. But it is of the essence of the operation that no element of hope or fear or ambition or disappointment should be allowed to interfere for one moment with the rigorous observation of, and obedience to, fact. Faith is indeed present, faith in the ultimate rationality of the universe which he is exploring; or, if the emergence of 'indeterminacy' makes that too strong a claim, faith at least in the rationality of the exploration. But it is a faith much more strictly controlled by evidence than would appear to him to be the case in much religious speculation.

No conclusion is to be regarded as final. Slowly, indeed, there may be built up a body of 'established findings', in the sense that for the time being further research is conducted on the provisional hypothesis of their reliability. But every fresh investigation or discovery may produce evidence which requires their re-examination, and possibly their rejection. Attention is focused all the time upon the *advance* of knowledge. '*Back* to the Bible', '*back* to the Ages of Faith', sounds an entirely alien note. The really significant truth is to be found, not in the first or the fifth or the fifteenth century, but in the new insights which have just emerged or are even expected to emerge round the next corner. The characteristic notes are provisional rather than absolute, new rather than old.

The full effects of concentration upon scientific method, as a solvent of religious belief, may be felt directly only by those exposed to it as an academic discipline. It is indeed to be remembered that they form a steadily increasing proportion of the educated section of the community. What is more, they constitute a very influential minority who possess an immense 'prestige value' as the exponents of what is too often regarded as 'the only reliable approach to verifiable truth'. But it is when we look at the implications of the expanded *power* which such knowledge puts into man's hands that the full force of the revolution becomes apparent.

It is to be seen at its maximum not in Europe but in Asia and Africa. In the West the gradual development over centuries has cushioned the violence of change by giving time for adjustment. In Asia and Africa the advance of centuries is taking place within decades. Within the span of one lifetime primitive tribal agricultural societies are being exposed to the full pressure of the technological machine age.

On the effects of this catastrophic process – political, economic, social, cultural, and religious – volumes have been written.* Here it is possible to note only one aspect, but an aspect of great significance from the point of view of a Christian evaluation. That is, to use the current jargon, the 'ambivalence' of the results. On the one hand there is the opening of men's minds to the possibility of liberation from disabilities and diseases, immemorially regarded as part of the natural, or indeed the divine, order. There is the dawning realization that man is not doomed to an endless round of poverty, dis-

---

* Cf. Heisenberg, *Physics and Philosophy* (Allen & Unwin, 1959), especially chapter 11, for a brilliant summary, which brings out in particular the significant shift of emphasis in twentieth-century physics.

ease, premature death. The power of fate can be broken.
Hard on the heels of this awakening sense of new knowledge
and power comes the demand for freedom to make use of
them. The nations of Asia and Africa want the white man's
science and technology: but they will no longer accept his
domination or exploitation.

All this the Christian conscience accepts with thankfulness,
if also with shame that it has been so long withheld, and is
even now often so grudgingly conceded. But there is another
side to the picture. Explosive forces of this kind are not selective in their impact. They do not leave untouched the
fabric of cultural and religious inheritance. The dissolution
of traditional beliefs, codes, and sanctions leaves whole
peoples without anchorage or authority or direction, at the
mercy of forces which they can neither understand nor control. Nor does the limited extent to which Christian faith has
been effective in controlling and directing the effects of the
parallel revolution in the countries of the West provide any
very secure ground for hope that it can meet the more radical
demands of a situation which has no centuries of Christian
civilization behind it.

When we turn to consider the working out of the scientific
and technological revolt in the more mature societies of the
West, the balance is perhaps even harder to strike. William
Temple used to speak of Christianity as 'the most materialistic of all religions'. That springs from its incarnational
principle, from the belief that the nature of God and of his
purpose for man have been most truly disclosed in a human
life. The life and teaching of Jesus make it abundantly clear
that the range of God's concern is as wide as daily life itself.
His desire for the good of his children includes everything
that makes for health, fulfilment, happiness. 'What God has
cleansed' (in the experience of one who spent most of his life
as a working craftsman) spiritually-minded persons are not
to call 'common or unclean'. There is no aspect of life at

home, at work, in social relationships of every kind, which cannot become the means through which God is glorified and his purpose furthered. That means of course that the Christian welcomes every achievement of social reform, made possible in large measure by the advance and application of scientific knowledge, which brings the good things of life, prosperity, health, educational opportunity, standing and recognition in the community, within the reach of increasing numbers. From this angle a comparison of the general level of human living in this country today with that which was common fifty years ago can only afford unmistakable evidence of the working of God's Spirit. Human beings have been increasingly set free from handicaps, disabilities, and privations which could not fail to stunt and warp their capacity to live as children of God.

And yet. The Litany, with that uncanny instinct for spiritual truth which it so often exhibits, couples the times of our 'wealth' (well-being) with those of our 'tribulation', as being equally occasions in which we need 'deliverance'. And alongside the 'materialistic' strain of which William Temple spoke, there is, deep rooted in the Gospel and in the Christian temper, the recognition that all these good things of life (and they *are* good things) are not in themselves the ultimate satisfaction, and can become the means by which men's eyes are blinded to its true character.

Drawing up a Christian profit and loss account for contemporary society is an undertaking which calls for a nice discernment. The credit side is on the whole easy enough to assess. It is the debits which are harder to reckon. We stand too close to some of the consequences of the growth of large-scale industry, and of the Welfare State itself, to make sure of the accuracy of our assessment. But some of the potential dangers are already apparent.

For increasing numbers of men and women their daily work is devoid of anything much in the way of meaningful satisfaction. Such phrases as 'the labour force' indicate a tendency towards mass groupings of workers in purely functional and often temporary associations which can easily diminish regard for personal rights and values. The shift of population and its reassembly in new and rootless aggregations can leave individuals and families with an acute problem of isolation. If the essence of the Christian Gospel is the fostering of the kind of community in which men can learn the lessons of mutual dependence, and by so doing develop their own powers of responsible living, then indeed there is ample opportunity for the rediscovery of that influence which, as we shall see in later chapters, is *par excellence* the Spirit of unity, of fellowship, and of cooperation.

But it is when we turn to the last of the three distinctive effects of the scientific revolution that the full weight of its impact begins to appear. Michael Foster's contrast between 'mystery' and 'mastery' might have been even more pointedly applied here. For the 'mastery' is by no means confined to man's expanding control of his material environment. The presuppositions and aims of the Natural Sciences have been taken over by what are now described as the Human Sciences. And the outcome is the deliberate assumption that man can deploy upon the study and control of his own make-up, his essential being, the same powers of observation and manipulation as have produced the miracles of chemistry and physics. The development of biology, psychology, and sociology is producing what its practitioners would like to regard as a 'science of behaviour'. Biology opens up the possibility of modifying the human embryo; psychological medicine is already capable of effecting radical transformations in the character and conduct of the individual. Anthropology and sociology advance the claim to be able to construct patterns of social environment which will exert an influence, hitherto regarded as the province of morality and religion, upon the creation of desirable attributes and attitudes. And already we are beginning to see, as with the advance of power, what a double-edged weapon this new sense of human autonomy can become.

On the one hand there is the unquestionable value of the new insights which psychology can throw upon our understanding and moral judgement in the matter of human responsibility. On the other there are the terrifying revelations of the possible effects of the abuse of such knowledge, when the resources and refinements of scientific advance are harnessed to the service of a devilish will to power.

The understanding of these new potentialities, and the capacity to use them, are still in the hands of a tiny minority. But the fact that they exist, and are known to exist, is already exercising a subtle but powerful influence upon the ordinary man's instinctive estimate of his standing in the scheme of things.

Mr Corbett, in the broadcast from which I have already quoted, added this comment.

Jesus spoke to men who sowed and reaped by hand, who tended the olive and the vine: men to whom disease and poverty were unalterable facts of life: men who knew only the authority of priests and tyrants. How would he have spoken to a technician living in a modern suburb, with a television set, a washing machine, and an old car: with the National Health Service and the Assistance Board at his elbow in times of distress: and with the industrial and political means to keep the powers that be attentive to his needs?

The point is well taken. And he might have gone on to add the further question: 'And how would such a man, and his wife, have responded to the message which he brought to them?'

Dr Oldham, in a notable passage in *Life is Commitment*,* speaks of this situation as 'man's coming of age'. And he insists on the crucial necessity to recognize and take reckoning with the true nature of the crisis. He writes:

* Op. cit., p. 19.

If Christianity is to have a meaning for men today it must make plain its attitude to this ambition to take on their own shoulders responsibility for their future. My own belief is that Christians must affirm unequivocally the rightness of man's desire to assume responsibility for the direction of his life and destiny. In the Christian view man is invested with a high dignity. If Christianity claims to be the bearer of a Word from God to man, that Word must be valid not only in the childhood of the race, but when man reaches the adult stage.

I believe that he is right, and that it is only when the Christian Church has faced and made this decision that it can claim the right to go further and confront men with the implications of such an assumption of responsibility. In particular it will have to think out afresh the significance of a conviction which is deeply rooted in its whole estimate of the nature of man. It is indeed a conviction which one might say starts in the Garden of Eden! Man *is* given the whole world of nature to enjoy and use. He is lord of the beasts. He may eat the fruit of all the trees in the garden – except one. What is the significance today of that one forbidden tree? Is it merely a relic from an age of primitive fear and superstition? Or does it stand as a symbol of something essential in man's relation to the order of the universe, a law of his own being which he disregards at his peril?

I have called this chapter 'The Religious Predicament'. Nobody could be more conscious than I am myself of the presumption of such a title, or of the inadequacy of what I have written to justify the choice. But it will have served its purpose if at least it has established one point.

We are seeking to understand the nature and activity of the Spirit of God. There is a famous passage in the Book of Wisdom in which it is said that 'the Spirit of the Lord has filled the world'. That is a truth too easily forgotten and ignored by those who would restrict his working to the sphere of the Church. Nor is it enough to say that the study of his working within the Church is the only safe clue to the discovery of his working in human life as a whole. Indeed the reverse may be true. It may well be that to limit our horizon in this way is to shut our eyes to some of the most significant evidence of his working. If we are to identify that evidence, still more if we are to help others to identify in their own experience a source of truth and power which as yet they have never associated with any idea of God, we must make ourselves sensitive to what is happening in the whole range of human life, to the forces which are shaping history, and to the insights which are prompting intellectual advance, artistic creation, and moral adventure. If this brief introductory sketch has served to set us thinking in this direction, it will have started us on the right road. Almost everything that it contains could be summed up in a memorable saying. 'If we want to hear what the Spirit is saying to the Churches, we must keep one ear to the ground.'

CHAPTER 2

Discerning the Signs of the Times

THE last chapter was an attempt to look at the impact upon human life of some of the great formative influences which within these last fifty years have increasingly shaped, and indeed dominated, man's ways of thinking and living. That the survey was partial and limited I am well aware. Some will, I expect, regard it as too pessimistic from the Christian point of view: they will say that it completely disregarded the evidence which is to be found in the life of the Church itself, with all the signs that can be detected of a real recovery in that life. Others will make the criticism that the view was far too short-sighted. At longest it glanced back as far as the seventeenth century; in the main it confined itself to the brief span of the first half of the twentieth. But that, they will say, is not the way to get a true perspective when you are considering the place of religion in human life. It takes no reckoning of the long ages of faith, of the deep roots which they have struck into human nature and civilization. These contemporary forces, powerful as they seem, and at the moment may be, will spend their force and ebb, as other revolutionary forces have done in the past. The Christian knows that he is meant to look at human history *sub specie aeternitatis*, and that gives a very different perspective.

With the first of these objections at least I hope that we may in some measure deal in the present chapter. For we turn now directly to look at the life of the Church in the setting of the contemporary world. And though I do not for a moment dispute the truth contained in the second criticism, I must say with frankness that I know how easily it can be misused to defend a very different temper, the temper which refuses to face the hard fact that the Church is living in the world as it is here and now, which forgets or ignores the difference between seeing the foreground against an eternal background, and shutting our eyes to the foreground altogether.

When I wrote that book twenty years ago I included something of a survey of the condition of Church life as I then saw it. It is interesting to look back at that estimate, and ask how much it needs to be revised. Let me at least say this. In my own experience those twenty years have included twelve spent in charge of a diocese, and with some participation in central Church affairs. From both parts of the experience I have learnt much for which I can never be sufficiently thankful; but I confess that it is to the former that I owe the greater debt. To have been allowed to see and share in the life of the Church as that is represented by the work of clergy and laity in almost every type of parish, town and country, is an experience at once humbling and heartening. The frustration springs much less from the failings of the men on the job than from the exasperating lack of imagination, elasticity, and effectiveness in the central organization of the Church.

How is the Church as a whole facing up to the task which confronts it in bringing home the Christian faith as 'reasonable, holy, and living' to the minds and consciences of men? Is its presentation in thought and worship and life such as to make men say, 'Oh, *that's* what this Christian faith means, is it? You've got something there'; to quicken their spiritual imagination by the demonstration of a 'holiness' which reflects the authentic note of the Gospels; to rouse them to action by making it plain that Christianity is geared to all the situations in the life of the community and of the world of which they themselves are already conscious as the points of need, danger, opportunity?

Setting a stiffish standard? Yes, of course. But that is what Christianity was meant to do since it began.

I said 'the Church as a whole': and it is worth pausing a

moment to reflect on the implications of those words, before
we embark on the main question.

So far as this country at least is concerned the basic pattern
of the Church's pastoral work has been shaped by the parochial system. How far that pattern corresponds to the realities
of a situation radically affected by the industrial and social
changes of the last hundred years is an open question. There
is indeed more than enough evidence to indicate the need for
some fairly drastic rethinking and consequent redeployment
of our resources of manpower. But even so it will remain true
that the direct influence of the Church's teaching and personal care will be mediated through local units in which
priests and people seek to work out the meaning of Christian
faith and living in terms of neighbourhood, or in some cases
occupational, needs.

But that work itself can never be fully effective unless it is
continually supported and fed by the work of others who in
one way or another perform the function of specialists. They
will exercise that function in a variety of ways. There will be
the theological scholars in the strict sense of the word, men
engaged upon the study of the Christian faith, carrying on the
work which has been continuous through the centuries, of
rethinking and reinterpreting the meaning of the original
revelation given in the Bible. Needless to say their work can
never be effectively done if it is done in a 'theological'
vacuum. For if one thing is clear, it is that the Christian faith
can never be rightly understood if it is regarded solely as a
body of truth existing in isolation over against the world of
'secular' knowledge. The function of theological scholars is
thus always a double one: the study and formulation of the
content of the 'given' faith, and the interpretation of that
content – one might almost say the cross-fertilizing of it – in
terms which take account of insights springing from the worlds
of philosophy, science, aesthetics, social studies. This in turn
means, of course, that the theologians must be in close personal

communication with the men and women who rank as their opposite numbers in the expertise of these other fields. Indeed it may often be the case that some of the most effective apologetic for the Christian faith will be done by those who are not themselves professional theologians, but who have by this means assimilated the results of first-rate theological thinking, which they in turn can *translate* into the language of philosophy, literature, drama, and the like.

There is one field in particular in which this work of cross-fertilization is urgently needed, the field of moral theology, the attempt to construct a coherent system of ethical judgements for the individual and for society, which derive their validity from the presuppositions of Christian beliefs. There is, it is safe to say, no sphere in which the Church speaks with less precision and authority. The great majority of its members are men and women who earn their living in the world of professional, industrial, and business life. Day by day they are confronted with moral problems arising out of the rapidly changing, and ever more complex, structure of that world. The ethical thinking of the Church has almost completely failed to keep pace with this development, and is therefore unable to make a Christian critique and judgement which is in any effective sense relevant to the actual situations with which it is asked to deal. This defect will not be made good until the moral theologians have spent a deal more time in the company of those who from inside experience can pose for them the real problems to which their technical knowledge must apply itself.

But there is one department of the Church's life in which the experts are called on to exercise an even more direct influence upon its pastoral office. That is, of course, the training of candidates for the ministry. Here above all is the need for men technically competent to transmit to the rank and file the material for a teaching ministry, *and* sufficiently aware of the strains and stresses of the 'non-theological' world to make that material relevant to the situations with which ordinands will be dealing when they go out to their work.

What has been said is sufficient to make it plain that in all these fields, parochial and specialist, the work of the Church includes the work of lay men and women. We shall have to return to this at length in later chapters. But here and now let the conviction be registered that, without that fruitful inter-play of lay and clerical thought and experience, the presentation of Christian truth, and experiment in Christian action, will remain one-sided, unbalanced, and ineffective.

To return to our main question. We can begin by recognizing that a large part of the task is in a sense a 'constant'. The maintenance of the worship of God and the training of Christians to take a full and intelligent part in that worship; the teaching of children, young people, *and* adults, the pastoral care whether of individuals or of a local community; these are the regular, unending responsibilities of the ministry, and of the lay men and women who work with them within the sphere of the parish or neighbourhood. If that is not being faithfully done, then no 'evangelistic campaigns', no 'liturgical experiments', no 'frontier work' in industry or elsewhere will achieve much of permanent value.

I called this basic work 'regular' and 'unending'. But not, I think, *unchanging*. 'Every scribe who has received instruction in the lore of the Kingdom is like a householder who brings out of his store things new and old.' It is a real temptation to us clergy to concentrate only on one form of the provision which we are expected to make for our households. Whereas, if the argument developed in the preceding chapter is sound, that can never be a full discharge of our duty. This 'religious predicament' which we were trying to explore is not a situation in which those outside the Church are living, while 'the faithful' inside are in some strange way insulated and immunized against it. *All* of us are living in this kind of world, whether we are more or less conscious of the fact. And indeed being less conscious of it may sometimes involve more serious consequences. For it may easily mean that our hold upon our faith has been more subtly undermined and weakened than we are aware, or should like to acknowledge. It may well involve that condition of a divided mind which in the last resort is the weakest foundation for effective action, and the weakest defence against relapse into indifference and infidelity.

In pleading therefore that the Church should take reckoning with this climate of our time, that it should consciously direct its spiritual strategy to meeting its needs and demands, one is not asking that the Church should direct its attention away from its primary task of shepherding the flock and caring for souls on to peripheral, if exciting, ventures into the no-man's-land which separates it from enemy territory. It is asking rather that the Church should explore in greater depth the real nature of its essential obligation, that it may discharge that more effectively.

Let us look again at the grounds on which Professor Toulmin had decided that, so far as he and others like him were concerned, they could no longer give religion any serious place in their view of life.

The Christian faith claims to offer men truth. It claims to set before them an understanding of life which makes sense in that it throws light on more of the dark places, and answers more of the riddles, than other explanations and interpretations. That famous passage which speaks of 'the light which lighteth every man, coming into the world' and 'shining in the darkness' always brings to my mind the image of a searchlight or a lighthouse whose beam sweeps the night. It does not altogether remove the darkness: it does not light up the whole scene. But wherever its beam rests it reveals in clear outline something which had hitherto been invisible or obscure.

But the plain fact is that for very large numbers of our contemporaries, that is no longer, or has never been, true. And they are not careless, indifferent, loose-living, frivolous folk. They are people of intelligence and responsibility, doing their work at high or humble levels as well as they can, and genuinely seeking for light which would enable them to do it better. They are to be found everywhere, in universities and schools, in medicine and law, in business management, in public service of every kind; and they are also to be found in offices, and on the shop floor, and at the sink. (Witness the evidence which comes in plenty to anyone who tries to expound the Christian faith over the radio.)

They just do not find in the Christian faith, *as they understand it*, a 'reasonable' view of life which they can accept without mental dishonesty or evasion, still less with a genuine sense of satisfaction. Many of them, like Mr Corbett, half wish they could. Why? Quite a number of the reasons are of course covered by those words 'as they understand it'. They don't. They have had little or no religious teaching in early years – or, which often matters more, in later. Their knowledge is precariously based on odd bits and pieces, newspaper articles, a talk on the air, the rather confused impressions derived from occasional attendance at Church worship. They have never been encouraged to make any sustained attempt to get a grasp of the faith as a coherent scheme of thought. Whose fault is that?

Some of them have fared better. They have had quite a good grounding; and maybe for a number of years felt reasonably secure and happy in believing. But their studies, philosophical, scientific, historical, or sociological, have raised difficulties which go far beyond some uncertainty as to the reliability of the Biblical record, and make even belief in God increasingly problematic.

Or it may be that experience of life, personal tragedy, or more likely perhaps the accumulated evidence of evil, confusion, and suffering in the world, has made it impossible to see in the Christian view of a world created, ordered, and

B

redeemed by God anything but a protective mechanism by which men have sought to shield themselves from cynicism and despair.

That there are other reasons of a different kind I well know. Absorption in material interests, the realization that seriously to accept Christianity is a hard option, the deliberate repudiation of all the values for which the Gospel stands; these are real facts. But it is never – repeat, never – legitimate for the Christian to *assume* that these are the real, though concealed, grounds for unbelief. A great deal of it does not spring in the main from these causes. It springs from the simple fact that men just *cannot* believe.

We have to ask ourselves what the Church is doing to wrestle with this genuine problem of unbelief. We shall have to come back to this question in the concluding chapters, in which some attempt will be made to see how a Church which had really recovered faith in a Spirit whose function is to lead men into all truth would be seeking to express that belief in its presentation of the Gospel. For the moment let us ask as honestly as we can how far, in the ministry of the word in our parishes, in the higher levels of theological thinking and writing, and in the preparation of the future clergy for their work, our aim is consciously directed to the task of vindicating the Christian faith as true, in terms of the actual difficulties of belief which are widely felt at many different levels of mental ability.

The second ground of Professor Toulmin's repudiation was that 'religion no longer dictates to us our ideas about morality and society'. Stated baldly like that, it is extremely doubtful whether this assertion is true. It depends perhaps to some extent on how much weight is attached to the word 'dictates'. Clearly the centre of gravity has shifted a long way since the centuries in which the Church was indeed the authority, the arbiter, whose rulings in spheres not only of private morality, but of public affairs, of commercial justice, and the administration of law were acknowledged and accepted. But it is still true that in a hundred ways our standards of morality, our recognition of what *ought to be* the principles of business and politics are subtly but really influenced and shaped if only by a residual Christian faith, and by a somewhat half-hearted maintenance of practices of prayer and worship.

But taking his assertion rather more broadly, there is no escaping the gravity of his charge. Over and over again in these last twelve years, as I have tried to make some assessment of the influences which shape the civic administration, the industry and commerce, the education, the public opinion of a great city, I have asked myself: where does the influence of the Church come into the picture? To what extent do men in positions of responsibility, in which they know that their decisions and actions affect for good or ill the lives of many thousands of their fellow-citizens, look to the Church for an informed and sympathetic understanding of their problems, and for at least some moral guidance which is really relevant to them? And I have directed the same question to myself – with far from flattering results.

It is not enough to reply, as some will do, that not a few of the men and women in question are faithful practising Christians who draw from their Church membership, their worship, and their prayers, much that supports them in facing the demands of the day's work. That, thank God, is true. But to adduce that as a satisfactory answer is only to show that the real issue has been missed. And indeed it is something worse than that. It is to substitute what might not altogether unfairly be called individual ambulance work for the true function of the Church: to be a community of people deeply committed to, and involved in, the moral ordering of the society of which they, and those outside the Church, are alike members.

It is worth reminding ourselves again of the various contributions which can and should be made from within the

Church as a whole. There is, as we saw, the need for men of
first-class academic ability who will undertake the work of
building up a new body of moral theology which draws its
material from the contemporary problems of state action and
industrial organization, so different from those which formed
the background of earlier formulations. That is a top-level
task which must be undertaken by experts. And again it must
be emphasized that such work is throughout a two-way
traffic in which the laity have an essential part to play.

But the same thing is needed at the humbler level of ordinary parochial ministration. Of how many of our churches can
it be said that they are the focus of a sustained exercise in
corporate thinking about the day-to-day problems which
men and women meet as they go about their business? In how
many cases is it true that the making of this Christian critique
of the trends of social, commercial, and political life is regarded as an essential part of preaching the Gospel and building up the faithful in their Christian understanding and
living?

It may well have seemed that so far we have been almost
exclusively concerned with what might be called the intellectual aspect of the Church's approach to its task. And we
may very properly be reminded that for many of those with
whom we are concerned that is not the natural, and will never
be the most fruitful, way of advance. The criticism is a fair
one. Many do indeed learn much of what the Christian faith
means, and grow in the capacity to translate that knowledge
into life, through regular sustained participation in worship.

And that of course only throws into sharper focus the
crucial importance of the *quality* of the Church's worship.
'God is Spirit: and those who worship him must worship him
in spirit and in truth.' None of us will ever fathom the full
meaning of that saying. But none of us can reflect on it at any
depth without seeing some of the demands which it implies.

Part, indeed a large part, of the value of worship is what

may be called its associative, its traditional, character. We do learn more of the meaning of worship, we do learn to worship better, through the repeated hearing of familiar words, and the repeated doing of familiar actions. Symbols, sacramental and un-sacramental, have in themselves a communicative and effective value. But is that all that is needed? Is the aim of worship simply to establish a kind of traditional pattern or rhythm in which we find ourselves increasingly at home, any disturbance of which we increasingly resent?

'In spirit and in truth.' Is our worship such that we, sometimes at least, come away from it feeling that we have been exposed to a pretty powerful draught, a breath of fresh air which is God's Spirit blowing away the cobwebs of convention and half-knowledge and prejudice and easy contentment with things as they are? Do we feel that there has been opened up for us a new vision of the nature of God, and, issuing from that, a new realization of the things for which, because God is what he is, he must be concerned?

Dr Vidler in one of his Windsor Sermons,* 'Would that you were cold or hot', has this passage:

In a living Church I should expect to find people, both young and old, showing quite an embarrassing interest in the Christian faith. I am always astonished by the way people go to Church, and say and sing and listen to the most extraordinary statements which I am sure they do not understand. But they hardly ever say, 'I jolly well want to know what that means. We must get the parson to explain what sense (if any) there is in that doctrine, in that passage of the Bible, in that hymn.' A Church that is hot is bursting with curiosity about the great mysteries of the faith; and is full of people who are determined to know what they are talking about.

I should expect to find the members of a Church that was becoming hot asking themselves how they could serve the whole of the community in which they are placed, whether it is a village or a town or part of a city. It is only lukewarm Churches that are indifferent to the quality of the public and social life in which they are set.

* *Windsor Sermons*, pp. 25, 26.

A Church that is alive is concerned about local government, about cultural and recreational activities, about people getting to know one another, and finding out how to live together the kind of life God wants us to live.

That particular sermon occurs in a section of the book which he calls 'Approach Shots'. I should reckon that he has laid that one stone dead.

We have asked some awkward questions. Are there any answers? Very definitely yes, even if, at this point, they can only be very briefly noted.

Intellectually the Church is becoming more alive to the formidable task which confronts it in validating the Christian faith as a live option in face of the challenge of philosophical, scientific, and historical criticism. We may still be woefully short of theological scholars: and the pressure on the time of the parochial clergy may leave them far too little opportunity and freshness of mind for serious reading. But on the one hand the publication within the last few years of such books as *Faith and Logic*, *Christianity and Paradox*, *New Essays in Philosophical Theology*, and *Theological Explanation* * is evidence that at the academic level the Christian faith is beginning again to be regarded as a matter worthy of serious consideration. And on the other, no one who has witnessed the enthusiasm with which the clergy, and especially the younger among them, respond to the stimulus of a solid clergy school, or to the opportunities provided by refresher courses such as those arranged by William Temple College, will feel unduly despondent.

On the side of social and industrial responsibility there are equally encouraging signs. The debt which the Church owes to the imagination and drive of the Bishop of Sheffield is one

* B. Mitchell (ed.), *Faith and Logic* (Allen & Unwin, 1957). R. W. Hepburn, *Christianity and Paradox* (Watts, 1958). A. Flew and A. MacIntyre (ed.), *New Essays in Philosophical Theology* (S.C.M., 1955). G. F. Woods, *Theological Explanation* (Nisbet, 1958).

which will never be fully repaid in this generation. The work which under his inspiration Canon Wickham* and his team have inaugurated has already had its effect all over the country. Much of it maybe is still somewhat haphazard and uncoordinated; but the experimental impulse is there, and there are signs at long last that there will be informed constructive direction from the centre.

But there is another indication of renewed livingness even more evident than those which I have mentioned. At first sight it might not perhaps appear to be directly relevant either to the theoretical task of vindicating the truth of the Christian faith or to the more practical one of relating that faith to the needs of life in industry and in society at large. But personally I am convinced, and that as a matter of direct observation, that it is one which indirectly at any rate has a very definite bearing upon both.

Behind all the critical questioning of the truth of religion, behind all the impatience with the irrelevance of much of the Church's activity to urgent human needs, there lies a deeper ground for scepticism. In the face of a world torn with racial, national, economic, ideological strife, what hearing can be expected for the preaching of a gospel of reconciliation by a Church itself as divided as the world to which it claims to speak? Wherever one turns, to the Church in India, a tiny minority confronting a vast non-Christian majority, to the Church in Africa facing the rising tide of racialism and the revolt against economic exploitation, to the Church on a housing estate seeking to create community out of disintegration, the same inescapable truth stares one in the face. How can Christians who have any regard for their Master's plain and unmistakable will continue in the wasteful folly and sin of division?

The history of the last half-century is at least a partial answer. Within these fifty years more has been done to set

* Now Bishop Suffragan of Middleton.

men's hearts and minds in the direction of penitence for disunity and of active effort towards removing it than in the
preceding four hundred.

Within this movement of the Spirit urging us towards the
recovery of unity two main strands can be clearly discerned.
There is first the recognition that the recovery can never be
achieved merely as an expression of emotional desire or
strategic expediency. It must be based on truth. Churches
separated from one another for many reasons: but inherent
in every schism or separation was an element of conviction,
on both sides, that some essential issue of Christian truth was
at stake. Until that conflict of conviction has been resolved
in a new understanding which does justice to the truth for
which each side believed itself to be standing, which indeed
reveals a deeper truth that neither of the two partial appre-
hensions was expressing, there can be no full and lasting
recovery of unity. One aspect therefore of the movement
towards reunion is the engagement in serious and persistent
theological conversation by which each side may hope to
present its own convictions more clearly and to understand
those of the other more sympathetically.

But theological discussion in a vacuum will never solve the
problem. There must be another kind of engagement in which
all concerned share in a common attempt to meet some of the
clamant needs of the world which are the responsibility of all
of them as Christian Churches. Here too the picture is encouraging. For during the post-war years there has been a
steadily growing expansion of Inter-Church Aid by which,
not only have urgent needs been met in country after country,
but the cooperating Churches have been drawn together in
an enterprise which has done much to break down misunderstanding and suspicion, and to demonstrate that the Spirit of
God is at least as truly revealed through *action* as through
theological discussion or even common worship.

It does not, I think, take much reflection to see the bearing of this question of unity upon the capacity of the Church to speak to men's condition. Is there one Christian faith to be proclaimed and taught, or are the Churches only rival ecclesiastical chain-stores, each claiming that its brand of detergent washes brighter or lighter or whiter than the rest? When some issue of political or social action arises which, on a true understanding, affects the moral well-being of a whole community, can the Churches speak with a single voice, or is it easy for unscrupulous agencies to play off one against another – or, more likely, to ignore them all?

If the argument of these two chapters has been sound, the inference to be drawn is not hard to see. The Church – indeed one may say religion itself – finds itself confronted with a situation of revolutionary change, the pace of which is such as to make adjustment to it of immense difficulty. And the difficulty is greatly increased by the fact that so many of the aspects of change are, as one might say, double-faced. They *appear* to be subversive of many of the established truths and values of religion: they present an outward front of sceptical criticism and embittered revolt. But on a deeper analysis many of them are seen to be the fruit of basic Christian impulses towards the discovery of truth and the establishment of righteousness, which should be hailed as allies rather than resisted as enemies.

Clearly what is needed in such a situation is a criterion of discernment at once radical and sensitive: radical in that it is prepared to welcome disconcerting views and happenings, sensitive in that it is able to identify, within the total impact of change, those elements which are truly expressive of the authentic Christian note – 'Behold, I make all things new'.

Is it too much to suggest that the power of which it is said 'He will guide you into all truth' and 'He will take the things which belong to [Christ] and make their meaning plain to you' is precisely the criterion of discernment which we need?

CHAPTER 3

Now – and Then

'I BELIEVE in the Holy Ghost, the Lord and Giver of life.'
There the words stand at the heart of one of the official creeds
of the Christian Church. How many of those who accept that
creed, still more who use it Sunday by Sunday in the Communion service, feel, as they say the words, that they are
affirming a truth to which they attach real and significant
meaning; that they are putting into words an experience
which they know to be the source of vitality, zest, inspiration,
joy in their own lives?

Other parts of the creed we can say with some measure of
conviction. We know something of what it means to affirm
our faith in a God upon whose creative and directing power
the whole of existence depends, yet who stands in relation to
every individual soul in an intimacy of knowledge and care
which is best described by the analogy of Fatherhood. We
know something of what it means to affirm our faith in one
in whom we believe that creative, directing love to be revealed, 'Christ, the wisdom of God and the power of God'.
But when it comes to the Spirit: well, we have been told that
the doctrine of the Trinity is the full expression of the Christian
apprehension of God – so we do our best; but it is a rather un-
convinced and unconvincing best.

This won't do. It stands to reason that if those words used
to describe the Spirit, 'Sovereign lord', the very power of
God, and 'Life-maker', continuous source and spring of creation, are true, then to go on saying them without understanding, without any feeling that they ring a bell, must mean that
our grasp of the faith is in that measure partial and defective.
In a sense that might not matter so greatly. There are, thank

God, many men and women in whom a very limited apprehension of the faith does not prevent some very effective
discipleship. But the trouble here goes deeper. For what these
words imply is that, by definition, the Spirit, the activity of
God through the Spirit, is the channel of communication by
which the very power to *live* effectively is made available to
us. And if that channel is blocked, it is doubtful how long
even the faithful discipleship will survive.

It is worth pushing this self-examination a little further.
How many occasions are there in the experience of the ordinary Church member on which the reality of the Spirit forms
the dominant theme in worship or instruction? I can only
speak from the experience of my own Church. Others must
make such correction and compensation as their traditions
require.

There is Whitsunday, with its familiar hymns, but its rather
baffling story of Pentecost, which suggests an occurrence not
in the least likely to recur in our own experience. There is the
Baptismal service, in which, among a good deal which is
obscure ('mystical washing away of sin', 'the burying of the
old Adam', and so on) there does indeed appear the explicit
prayer for the gift of the Holy Spirit to the child. But it may
be permissible to wonder how much, even with careful preparation beforehand, an average group of parents and god-
parents makes of this prayer, or of the assurance that it has
been answered which follows later in the service.

There is Confirmation. Here indeed we might feel is the
great opportunity. The pundits may argue interminably as to
the precise relation of the gift of the Spirit in Baptism to that
in Confirmation. But no one who studies the service carefully,
or still more forms one of those almost invariably reverent and
expectant congregations who attend it, can fail to realize that
it is the bestowal of the Spirit, through prayer and the laying
on of hands, which constitutes the heart of it. And yet, if I am
to be honest, I must confess that time and time again when I

have longed to base the address on one of those many great
New Testament passages, in which the Spirit shines and lives,
I have hesitated, because, perhaps faithlessly, I have doubted
whether the congregation, or even the candidates, would
have had that grounding in the New Testament background
which would make such an approach relevant and meaningful. And one is left – again perhaps to one's shame – wondering: now just what do they think they have received? What
do they hope may happen as the result of it?

There is Ordination. But this is for the tiny minority who
are called to this special office and function. We may indeed
thank God for the steady growth of parochial attendance at
Ordinations. But one suspects that, in spite of many admirable sermons to the contrary, the emphasis falls in their minds
mainly upon the 'setting apart' of men for a priestly ministry.
How much more significant would that be, how much more
would it convey of the true nature of the Church, if at their
Confirmation they had heard the true intention of that service expressed in some such words as 'Receive the Holy Spirit
for the office and work of a lay member in the Church of God'.

There are not many more such occasions. Is it any wonder
if the average Churchman tends to regard the Spirit as an
occasional, exceptional, even slightly abnormal element in
the faith and life of the Church? He may indeed, if he is given
now and then to venturing outside the fold, find himself confronted with some surprisingly vivid evidence of a type of
religion in which the Spirit appears to play a much more
dramatic part. Bishop Lesslie Newbigin* has reminded us
that the Catholic and Protestant traditions by no means ex-
haust the full content of Christian witness either historically
or in our own day. But our average Churchman, straying
occasionally into a place of Pentecostalist worship, may well
come away almost more perplexed than before. He may likely
enough feel that what he has met with strikes, and even

* *The Household of God* (S.C.M., 1953), chapter 4.

shames, him by its vitality. But he will not perhaps feel too
sure that for him at least this could ever provide the 'bread-
and-butter' religion which will form a staple diet from
Monday to Saturday.

And then we turn to the New Testament. If we are really
conscientious we can sit down and read steadily through it
with pencil and paper at hand to note down the references to
the Spirit and his working. If we are lazier we can let a concordance do the work for us. We shall quickly be struck by the
fact that the spread of these references is very uneven. In the
Gospels, particularly in the first three, they are surprisingly
scanty; in John they are more frequent, though here they tend
to group themselves like little nebulae or clusters, in certain
chapters. It is when we pass to Acts and Paul's letters that the
flood sets in. Moulton and Geden's *Concordance to the Greek
Testament* lists seventy-two such references in Acts, and close
on a hundred and fifty in Paul's letters. Clearly something has
happened.

But of course mere statistical evidence of this kind only
takes us a very little way. It is not until we begin to dig into
the evidence, to study the kind of thing which happened, and
the kind of explanation which men give of it, that the impression forces itself upon us that this 'Spirit', whoever or
whatever he or it may be, is the clue to the plot of the drama.

In this chapter and the three which follow it we shall be
trying to study that evidence. There are books of scholarship
(some of them listed in the Bibliography) in which the New
Testament theology of the Spirit is fully set forth. Our object
here is a simpler one, to try to recapture something of the
background of the experience of which that theology is the
formulated expression. And we may start, by way of an
aperitif, with a few samples, chosen at random from Acts,
which may serve to whet our appetite for more.

Now it happened that while Apollos was in Corinth, Paul crossed
the highland in the interior and came down to Ephesus, where he

met some new converts. He said to them, 'Did you receive Holy Spirit when you became Christians?' They answered, 'We never so much as heard that there was such a thing as Holy Spirit.' 'Whatever kind of baptism was it that you received?' he asked them. 'It was the baptism of John Baptist', was their reply. So Paul explained to them that John's baptism had been a preparatory baptism of repentance (its emphasis had been on the break with the past). It pointed beyond itself to one who was to follow, Jesus, who would, as John himself had said, baptize with a very different baptism, of Holy Spirit and fire. When they heard this, they were baptized into the name of Jesus. And when Paul had laid his hands upon them, they broke out into ecstatic speech and prophecy (Acts 19:1–6).

It is an odd little story. Why was it thought worth preserving? Scholars will tell us that it affords an interesting bit of evidence for the continuance of something like a John Baptist sect. Its real point is, I think, less antiquarian and a good deal more cogent.

'Did you receive Holy Spirit when you became Christians?' Why is that somewhat brusque question Paul's first remark to them? There can surely be only one answer. They didn't look as if they had. Something was missing that ought to have been there, something that men were beginning to look for as a distinctive mark of those who had had the characteristic vitalizing experience of becoming Christians. (Workers in the Church in India or Africa sometimes say that you can tell the Christians in a village by the look on their faces.) Their answer confirmed his doubt. They had never so much as heard of this experience. So he took steps to have things put right. They were properly received (no doubt after some further instruction) into the Christian community. 'And when Paul had laid his hands upon them, they broke out into ecstatic speech and prophecy.' We shall see later on that this was not then, any more than it would be today, regarded as the most desirable evidence of the Spirit's influence in the life of Christians. But there is no mistaking the fact that something had happened. A spring, as it were, was released; there was an inner response to the touch of a divine power. Does anything comparable happen to most of us at Confirmation? And would it be a good thing if it did? It sets one thinking.

So they travelled through Phrygia and the territory of Galatia, because they were prevented by the Holy Spirit from doing any preaching in the province of Asia. When they came to Mysia they tried to cross into Bithynia: but the Spirit of Jesus said No. So they by-passed Mysia and came down to the coast at Troas. There one night Paul had a vision. He saw a man from Macedonia standing and appealing to him with the words 'Come over into Macedonia and help us there'. And as soon as Paul had seen this vision he made urgent plans to get over into Macedonia, convinced that God had made it plain that we were to carry the Gospel to them too (Acts 16:6–7).

Forget the geography and the maps of 'Paul's missionary journeys'. Look at the story in another way. These men were on tour, with their plans carefully made for mission preaching in what they believed to be strategic centres. Something went wrong. It may have been that the road was washed away: or the authorities had refused them entry. Anyway they changed their plan and tried a fresh cast. And again the same thing happened, only this time apparently in an even more de- cisive way. And as they sat round their fire in the evening on the road side, one of them said – 'Look here! This is the second time that we have been held up. I believe there's more in this than meets the eye. I believe we weren't *meant* to do either of the things we had planned. There must be something else which our Master has in mind for us.' So they changed course again and found themselves at Troas. And there they dis- covered what they were meant to do. They were to carry the Gospel into Europe.

A man called Ananias, with his wife Sapphira, sold some pro- perty, and with his wife's collusion kept back part of the price he got for it, and brought the rest and deposited it in the common pool which was supervised by the Apostles. And Peter said to him,

'Ananias, why did you let Satan put into your mind this idea of cheating the Holy Spirit by keeping back part of the price? While the land was yours it was yours: and when you'd sold it you were at liberty to do what you liked with the proceeds. What induced you to yield to a dirty trick like this? You haven't cheated men: you've cheated God' (Acts 5:1–4).

The background of the story is what is sometimes inaccurately described as an early Christian experiment in communism. Wealthier members of the community were encouraged to pay into a pool for the benefit of the poorer. There was no obligation so far as we know to contribute the entire proceeds of any sale of property. Ananias could quite honourably have made a part payment on the ground that he couldn't afford more. But he wanted to have it both ways: to keep part of the cash for himself, *and* to appear to be doing what more generous or wealthier donors were doing. Peter saw through the deception. Maybe he remembered a remark that had been made to him some years ago when he had put a question about the reward that would be coming to people who 'gave up all': his conscience had been a bit sensitive on that subject ever since. And he turned on this miserly humbug with a rebuke which laid bare the full extent of his deception. 'You haven't cheated men, you've cheated the Holy Spirit, you've cheated God.'

Put these three bits of evidence together and reflect on them. They make it plain that into the life of this little Christian community there had come a new influence which was felt to exercise a decisive control in a variety of ways.

It operated in the lives of individuals. Men and women as they accepted the new faith and came into membership of the Christian fellowship might expect – might indeed be expected – to experience not only a definite break with the past but a positive influx of spiritual power and enthusiasm. Nor was that just a temporary inspiration such as may frequently be seen in the early stages of a conversion. It lasted. It showed itself, as we shall have occasion to see, in a variety of forms. In the particular instance which we have considered it showed itself in the form of a strong sense of being directed. Often enough that direction might in the first instance take a negative form. And that is an experience which we ourselves know. We find a road which we had planned to take closed in our face. We try another; the same thing happens again. Eventually we reach a point at which we say, 'Oh! I see, that's why those plans didn't work. God had something else up his sleeve.'

But it operated also on a different scale. This influence was found at work at the heart of the corporate life of the community. That is of course the point of Peter's exposure of Ananias. 'You thought', he says, 'that you could get away with a bit of sharp practice which, if you condemned it at all, you would only have condemned as a slightly anti-social act. But in the Christian community an anti-social act is never only that. It is an offence against the inner spirit of the community which gives it loyalty and mutual trust and cohesion, a denial of the very truth which it is trying to live out in its Christian solidarity. And that mutual trust and responsibility are the gift of God's Spirit, his power at work in the common life.'

In the light of all this, we can come back for a moment to Pentecost. Perhaps it is rather clearer now why we did not start with that. For now it should be possible to see why they attached the cardinal importance which they did to the moment at which they had first become corporately conscious of the release among them of this power. And at this point it is necessary to clear up what is pretty certainly a misunderstanding on the part of the author of Acts. In the opinion of scholars the 'speaking with tongues' is not an abnormal endowment with the capacity to speak a hitherto unknown foreign language. It is the first instance of that 'ecstatic speech' which we met in the story of the Ephesian converts.

It is a phenomenon which has occurred constantly in religious revivals throughout Christian history, even as late as the nineteenth century.* Obviously that particular expression of the Spirit's working, which indeed Paul had to curb pretty drastically in his congregations, is not the really significant thing about the story, or about the event. It is the power to 'speak boldly', to declare 'the wonderful works of God', which is the thing that matters.†

Before we go on to examine in more detail the evidence of which these stories are only samples, it will repay us to get a clearer picture of this first Christian community within which the Spirit was at work.

Dr Vidler in an illuminating passage in his Cambridge lectures *Christian Belief* ‡ has called attention to 'certain facts which were in the world at the end of the first century, but which were not there when it began'. One may paraphrase his statement of the case something like this.

Imagine yourself on a fairly extended visit to the eastern Mediterranean towards the end of that century. The ship calls at a number of ports, and it is possible for passengers, if they wish, to stop off and spend some time for instance at Corinth or Smyrna or Ephesus. If you had merely made for the best hotel, and spent your time, as tourists often do, between that and the luxury shops, you would have seen – well, all that tourists often do see. But if you had a taste for getting off into the small streets round the docks, better still if you had friends on the spot who knew the place really well from inside, you might have seen much more. They might have told you that among all the sects and cults which flourished

* Cf. R. A. Knox, *Enthusiasm* (O.U.P., 1950), chapter 22.

† It is worth noting that Harnack and others distinguish two sources underlying Acts 1–5 and suggest that there are two parallel accounts of Pentecost, the earlier *c.* 4:23–31, the later *c.* 2:1–47. There are significant differences between the two. Cf. F. J. F. Jackson and K. Lake, *Beginnings of Christianity* (Macmillan, 1926–33), vol. 2, pp. 126 ff.

‡ *Christian Belief* (S.C.M., 1950), chapter 3.

in the city, there had recently appeared a new one. They might have made it possible for you to join its members at one of their meetings for fellowship and worship. You might even, if you were singularly fortunate, have been present on an occasion when they read aloud a circular letter which had recently reached them from a man called Paul.

If you had had the time to cultivate their acquaintance and observe them with sympathetic understanding, certain impressions would probably have formed themselves in your mind. They seemed to be people who on the whole kept themselves to themselves. They didn't mix much in the ordinary round of civic affairs or public amusements. Indeed, they took rather a poor view of a good deal that went on around them. And yet they were, curiously enough, very *inclusive* in their membership. You noted in their gatherings representatives of racial, religious, and cultural groups who would hardly be on speaking terms outside: the morally exclusive Jew, the somewhat superior Greek, even an occasional Roman official, rubbing shoulders with the down-and-outs from the docks. (It was rather like finding members of the Nationalist Government or wealthy Indian merchants from Durban mixing with the Bantu population of Sophiatown.)

They were, with few exceptions, not people of any great standing or influence in the life of the community, 'not many wise, not many mighty' – 'not many respectable', Celsus would have added. And yet there was something about them for which that hard-worked word 'dynamic' seemed to be the appropriate description. They used strange language about 'possessing the powers of the age that is to be', and it didn't seem to be just a phrase. They exhibited a mental and spiritual vigour which was unmistakable; after all, they must presumably have understood some parts of Paul's letters. And they constantly spoke of 'hope' and 'faith' and 'joy' in a world which for the most part was – like our own today – noticeably lacking in those qualities.

They seemed to live under a pretty strict discipline. They didn't go much to the theatre or the games. They recognized a much more severe standard of morality than most of their neighbours. They seemed to take a curious delight in speaking of themselves as 'slaves'. (A number of them *were*; so they knew what they were talking about.) But they added 'of Jesus the Messiah'. And yet at the same time another word which was constantly on their lips was 'liberty', 'freedom'. 'The glorious freedom of the sons of God' was something which clearly meant something real to them. They felt, and looked, like men who had been delivered from some kind of bondage. If you had asked them to tell you something more about this 'secret society' to which they belonged, they would very likely have said that they had been nicknamed 'Christians', 'Messiah's men'. And if you had asked them what that meant, they might have replied in words which one of their leaders had used in a speech some years earlier.

You all know the story which got abroad and spread through all Judea, starting in Galilee, after John's baptism preaching, the story of Jesus who came from Nazareth. It told how God anointed him with Holy Spirit and with power. He went about doing good and healing all who were under the devil's power: for God was clearly with him. We ourselves can bear witness to all the things he did both in the country of the Jews and in Jerusalem itself. They killed him: they hung him on a cross. But God raised him from the dead on the third day and allowed him to be seen, not indeed by everybody, but by some of us whom God had chosen as witnesses, who actually ate and drank with him after he had risen from the dead (Acts 10:37–41).

And so, starting as indeed the New Testament itself starts from these little underground movements, we come round to their source in the Gospels. We have already noted that the references to the Spirit in the Gospels, especially in the first three, are surprisingly scanty. Professor C. K. Barrett in his book *The Holy Spirit and the Gospel Tradition* * has made a full

* S.P.C.K., 1947.

and masterly study of all the relevant evidence, and has discussed with great thoroughness the question which inevitably emerges from such a study. Why, when the life and thought of the early Church, out of which the Gospels sprang, was steeped in the influence of the Spirit, is there so little in their record of the life of Jesus himself to account for this?

The answer, very briefly summarized, would seem to be something like this. The world into which Jesus came was a world in which the belief in 'spirits' and their power over human life was rife. And because of that, men's minds were only too readily attuned to such phenomena as 'spirit possession' and to the means, exorcism, magic, and the like, of dealing with them. In a few pages of Acts we meet with Simon Magus and Elymas the sorcerer, a woman ventriloquist at Philippi, and the seven sons of Sceva who claimed to possess powers of exorcism; and the Gospels themselves provide ample proof of the widespread readiness to fasten on a 'miracle' of healing or exorcism as the really significant evidence of 'spiritual' power. The prime concern of Jesus was to dissociate his own mission and power from a preoccupation of men's minds which could only distract them from his true purpose: to demonstrate in word and act the true nature of God's Spirit at work in himself. Hence the evident reluctance to allow prominence to be given to his healings, the fact that there is no subsequent mention in his teaching of the experience which had come to him at his baptism, the absence of any reference to 'visions' or other ecstatic phenomena. His whole object was to salvage the understanding of how God's Spirit works, and how his presence may be known, from superstitious and degrading misrepresentation. It was to demonstrate in terms of ethical quality what 'holy' Spirit means. It was when, and only when, he had by his life and death vindicated that truth, that the power of the Spirit could, as it were, be liberated in full force. There is an illuminating hindsight realization of this fact in the strange comment in the Fourth Gospel: 'For as yet there was not Spirit (Spirit was not yet operative), because Jesus had not yet been glorified' (John 7:39). It was not until men had seen the true meaning of 'glory' in a life so utterly unlike the ordinary sense of glory, that the power released by it could become effective.

But it is just this very fact which makes the references which are to be found of such peculiar significance. Put them together in terms of the experience which they must have conveyed to those who had witnessed the events to which they refer. They had seen him come to Jordan to receive baptism from John. They may, or may not, have been aware of any special revelation which had come to him at that moment. The evidence is uncertain. But they saw him go off by himself, and for a time he disappeared altogether. Later on, when they came to know him, he told them something of what his baptism and his subsequent disappearance had meant. 'Why did you go off alone like that?' 'I knew that the moment for which I had been waiting had come.' 'How did you know it?' 'How does a man know that kind of thing? What name does one give to that inner compulsion, that certainty that God has something to say to one, something which one must wrestle with by oneself? The Spirit drove me into the desert.'

They knew that he was speaking the truth. They had seen him come back 'in the power of the Spirit': look and word and action confirmed it. And the rumour of it had spread like wild-fire.*

Only now and again had he spoken of it. On an early occasion when he had attended the weekly worship in the synagogue he had been asked to choose the passage for reading and to make the usual commentary on it. He had deliberately selected a passage from Isaiah which in the ears of the hearers would carry an unmistakable meaning: 'The Spirit of the Lord is upon me, because the Lord has anointed me to

---

* Matt. 3:1-17; 4:1. Luke 3:15-22; 4:1, 14-15.

preach good tidings to the poor: he has sent me to proclaim release to captives, and sight to the blind, to set free the wounded and oppressed, to proclaim the Lord's year of favour' (Isa. 61:1–2). And then, with everyone's attention riveted on him, he had added quite quietly, 'You know what that means: you know that that is what our nation has hoped for and clung to for centuries. Well, it has come.' *

They had seen this implicit claim substantiated by the things he did and said, and by the authority with which he did and said them. Of course the authorities had hotly challenged it. 'Possessed by God's Spirit, indeed! It's easy to see where he gets his power from. Make friends with the prince of the demons, and of course you can control his subordinates.' There had been one terrifying moment when he rounded on this misrepresentation and exposed it for what it was. This calling white black, this attributing to the devil what was unmistakably the work of God, was a sin against the Holy Spirit, a repudiation of the very power of moral and spiritual discernment by which men can distinguish good from evil. To do that is the final blasphemy. For that there can be no forgiveness.†

Very occasionally there had been a lifting of the veil. There had been a moment of intense spiritual exaltation when he had laid bare the inmost secret of his unfailing sense of communion with God. 'I thank thee, Father, Lord of heaven and earth, that thou hast hidden these things from the wise and prudent and hast revealed them to babes. ... All things have been committed unto me by my Father. ...' ‡

They had watched as his chosen course of action, and the teaching by which he vindicated it, led him to his death. Looking back on the events afterwards they could see that that had been bound to happen. But at the moment it had felt like the end. As he hung there, his triumphant enemies had

* Luke 4:16–21.   † Luke 11:14 ff.; 12:8–10.
‡ Luke 10:21–2.

seemed to call his bluff: 'If you really are the son of God, come down from that cross: seeing's believing'; and this time he had no answer.

Of course if it *had* been the end, there would have been no 'underground movement' to tell the story.

CHAPTER 4

A Fellowship of Holy Spirit

'If it had been the end there would have been no "underground movement" to tell the story.' That is the clue to all that follows. The witness to the spirit of Jesus present and potent in the life of the Christian community would be, to my mind, inexplicable unless the black despair of Good Friday had been lifted by an event which, however we may seek to interpret its exact nature, had convinced his friends past any manner of doubting that the death had *not* been the end.

The preliminary sketch in the last chapter gave us an inkling of what the release of the Spirit's power meant to the first Christian community. We proceed now to consider in more detail the nature of that experience as it is described for us mainly in Paul's letters.

It is worth emphasizing – though the point is by now more familiar than it used to be – that they are *letters*. No one would have been more astonished than Paul himself, if he could have realized that nineteen hundred years later these letters which he had dictated, not infrequently in haste for dispatch by road or ship, had become the sacred scriptures of a world-wide Church, and had been the subject of countless volumes of commentary and exposition. And it is nothing short of a disaster that for very large numbers of Christians they have become to all intents and purposes a closed book – classified in the catalogue as 'Dogmatic Theology: for advanced students only'. Of course they are not always easy reading. That is due in part to the fact that the background of life and thought which they reflect is in many ways very different from our own; partly to the fact that they are the product of one of the ablest minds of the ancient world wrestling with questions to some of which nineteen centuries of Christian thought have found no final answers. But they are *not* unintelligible, still less irrelevant. They deal with issues which go to the very heart of Christian faith and conduct. And indeed, though at first sight it may seem a strange thing to say, they are in a real sense *more* apposite to our own needs than the Gospels themselves. For they are the record of men painfully working out the meaning and implications of what had been given in the life and death and resurrection of Jesus, without the help of his personal presence as an immediate point of reference. They are in fact an illustration of men working under the influence of his Spirit.

Fortunately this grave handicap to the full understanding and use of the New Testament has been largely removed thanks to the inestimable benefit conferred on our generation by the genius of J. B. Phillips's paraphrase translation. Whether one reads it alongside the Authorized or Revised Version or the original Greek, one never fails to recognize how constantly he brings out meanings and connexions left obscure in the earlier English versions, and illuminates with a fresh and stimulating turn of phrase passages the very familiarity of which had staled them. With *Letters to Young Churches* * in his hands, and the readiness to do a bit of serious study, anyone can now hope to tackle 'the Epistles'.

Among the characteristics of the first Christian congregations noted in Dr Vidler's survey was that of a surprising inclusiveness. Something had come to them which had taken the edge off the sharp cleavages of race, culture, and religion which in the setting of life outside the Church would have made personal relations of understanding and mutual respect difficult, if not impossible. It is not of course to be supposed that this process of growing together was automatic or easy. From the very start there is evidence that there were signs of friction between 'the Grecian Jews' and 'the Hebrews'

* J. B. Phillips, *Letters to Young Churches* (Bles, 1947).

(Acts 6:1). The same tensions made themselves felt as the Christian movement spread into the world of the Dispersion. The whole story of Paul's missionary work in Asia Minor and Greece is marked by those recurrent antagonisms, originating usually in the indignation aroused in Jewish minds by his conviction that the Gospel was meant for all, and that its refusal by Jews opened the way for its presentation to the Gentiles.

The real inwardness of the problem of welding these diverse elements into a fellowship, in which mere tolerance would be replaced by a deep sense of common sharing in a new life, can be illustrated from a consideration of two famous antitheses which figure so largely in Paul's presentation of the Gospel. They are the antitheses between 'life in the Spirit', and 'life under the Law', and between 'life in the Spirit' and 'life according to the flesh'.

The first is the problem for the Jewish side of the Christian community. At the heart of Judaism as it existed in the first century there stands the religious man's reverence for, and devotion to, the Law. For him religion was the keeping of the Law. And before we hastily condemn that equation as 'mere legalism', let us remember that the Torah meant infinitely more to the devout Jew than a code of legal regulations; one has only to read Psalm 119 to catch something of the temper which its study inspired. And let us also realize that it was largely this which had preserved two things of quite incalculable value amid the moral and intellectual welter of Greco–Roman decadence: a rigid monotheism, and obedience to a stern and exacting moral standard. It has been truly remarked that 'the moral stamina of the Jew was almost the only piece of firm ground left in the swamp of the Levant'.

Even a very casual reading of the Gospels is enough to bring out the extent to which Judaism was dominated, so far at least as its Pharisaic side was concerned, by this demand. It was on the rock of his refusal to be bound by the strict literal interpretation of the Law's requirements that the irrecon-

cilable split between Jesus and his opponents occurred. It was
his reinterpretation of the true nature of Sabbath observance,
of the nature of defilement and cleanness, that brought down
upon him the fiercest accusations of undermining the whole
fabric of morality.

But the real character of his refusal to accept legalism as the
truth of religion, a refusal as vigorously sustained by Paul, the
converted Pharisee, is not to be found in any mere satirizing
of the extravagances of casuistry into which a slavish obedience to it had led. The root lies far deeper.

The identification of religion with 'law-keeping' carries
within itself the seeds of a terrible perversion. For once religion is thus identified with the observance of regulations, it
becomes externalized, reduced to a minutely scrupulous
doing of works. And from that it is not a long step to the
position in which a man begins to regard his religion as a
matter of book-keeping. You open an account with God. On
the credit side are entered the good deeds, the attendance at
worship, the regular prayer, the almsgiving, the works of
charity. There are entries of course on the other side also; for
many who fall into this mistake are men of sensitive conscience, with a real sense of sin. But the damage has been
done. For it is possible, when the reckoning is made, to
strike a credit balance. And even that is not the real danger.
The disastrous mistake is the growth of the belief that it is
possible for the religious man to earn God's favour, and that
that is what religion is.

From that springs a crop of evils. Self-righteous satisfaction, contempt for others whose performance may not seem
to equal our own, though we know nothing of their struggles
in circumstances far less favourable than ours. 'God, I thank
thee that I am not as other men are. ...' Unless recognized
and checked, it leads inevitably to one of two end-situations:
moral self-deception and the blinding of the conscience to
truth; or complete disillusionment and despair. With the

poorer type of Jew it led to the former. With the finer, including Paul himself, to the latter. And the story of that bitter
awakening can be read in that most revealing of all confes-
sions, the seventh chapter of Romans.

The escape from this impasse is to be found in the realization – and it can be, as it was for Paul himself, a shattering
experience – that one has got one's religion exactly the wrong
way round. Religion does not consist in earning God's favour
by being good. It consists in realizing that one is not good, and
accepting the forgiving love of God which is the only thing
which can make one a little less bad.

The sense of deliverance from this hell of despair, which
came to Paul through the discovery of the truth, runs like a
golden thread through all his letters. Here is one illustration:

But now, quite apart from Law, we have a demonstration of God's
righteousness [what he means by righteousness, the kind of righteousness which reflects his own nature]. There is indeed evidence of
it in the Law and the prophets [the writings of the old dispensation],
but it does not come from them. It is a righteousness which comes
from God, and it comes as a response to trusting Jesus Christ. All can
have it who do so trust: for there is nothing to choose between any
of us. We have all missed the way, and fallen short of the glory which
God meant us to see and share in himself. And the only way in which
we get set right again is by humbling ourselves to accept, free gratis
and for nothing that we can do to earn it, the forgiveness offered us
in Jesus Christ (Romans 3:21–4).

To have passed through that experience is to have been
delivered from what can only be called slavery, the slavery
which comes from a hopeless attempt scrupulously to obey
an infinity of regulations, the worse slavery which consists
in trying to 'establish our own righteousness', to satisfy ourselves that we are satisfying God. It is to have passed from the
status of a slave to the relationship of a son.

It is those whose lives are directed by the Spirit of God who know
what it means to be sons of God. For the Spirit which you received
is not a spirit of slavishness, with its inevitable attitude of cringing

fear. It is a spirit which makes us realize that we are sons, and so able to call God by his true name, Father. The Spirit itself [the Greek is neuter] confirms the certainty in our own spirits that we are children of God (Romans 8:14–16).

It was an experience of this kind which alone made it possible for the typical devout Jew to exchange his old 'holier than thou' attitude for a humble recognition that his spiritual need was just like anybody else's, and so to find himself at home in the company of those with whom before he would never have associated, a member with them of 'a fellowship of Holy Spirit'.

But it does not take much reflection to realize that to preach this kind of Gospel had its risks. It provoked exactly the same kind of bitter – and sincere – criticism from the orthodox as that which Jesus himself had aroused. 'Selling the pass, sacrificing principle, hob-nobbing with Gentiles.' (It is not difficult to think of contemporary situations in which similar phrases are current.) And indeed they were real dangers. To tell people that they were 'no longer under the Law' was to open a rather too attractive prospect of liberty, if not of licence, to weaker brethren. And there were times when such people had to be reminded that in throwing off the yoke of the Law they had not been granted freedom from obedience to *any* master. They had only exchanged the wrong master for the right one. They had indeed been set free from the legalism which could never offer release from sin. But it was 'the law of the Spirit of life in Christ Jesus' which had done it. And the demands of that law set a standard which, as their Master had warned them, 'exceeded the righteousness of the Scribes and Pharisees'.

It made things difficult sometimes with the Jewish side of the new Church. But it raised equal, if not greater, problems with others.

That dreadful first chapter of Romans in which Paul lets loose the full force of his vocabulary to describe the moral rottenness of the pagan world, could be illustrated a dozen times over from Juvenal, Martial, and the rest. And that was the background out of which not a few of the non-Jewish converts had come. Like other converts in our own time they had not found it easy to leave their past behind them on the door-step. If anyone entertains any illusions about 'the ideal Christianity of the early Church', the first letter to Corinth should be sufficient to dispose of them. 'Fornicators, idolators, adulterers, guilty of unnatural vices, thieves, spivs, drunkards, scandal-mongers, extortioners. That is what some of you used to be' (1 Cor. 6:9–11).

If the Jew had to be rescued from bondage to the Law, the Gentile stood in even greater need of similar deliverance from 'the flesh'. With the former it was a question of showing him that his better self could be the enemy of his best. With the latter it was a question of bringing home to him the degraded quality of his worst.

Volumes have been written on the Pauline psychology of 'flesh' (*sarx*), 'soul' (*psyche*), and 'spirit' (*pneuma*). For our purpose we shall, I believe, be near enough to the truth if we paraphrase the two former as 'our unredeemed animal nature', and 'our unredeemed intellectual nature'. (The identification is not wholly satisfactory, but, broadly interpreted, it may serve.) Neither of these is, on the Christian view, inherently evil; for both are parts of the total endowment which is God's gift; and a more enlightened insight, the fruit of modern psychological research, has wholesomely modified and corrected some of the more sweeping condemnations of both pre- and post-Reformation estimates.

But no such modification has shaken the Christian conviction, based on a realistic observation of experience and self-knowledge, that both these aspects of our nature, as we know them in their 'natural' state, are 'corrupt', vitiated by a taint or distorted by a twist, which makes it impossible for them to be what they are meant to be.

For an understanding of what Paul means when he speaks of 'the flesh' we have only got to look at the list which he gives of its 'works': 'sexual vice, filthy-mindedness, sensuality, idolatry, magic, quarrels, dissensions, envy, anger, rivalry, factiousness, murder, bottle parties, petting parties, and such like' (Gal. 5:20–1). We realize indeed, at a glance, that to our mind today such a list could hardly be brought within the limits of 'our unredeemed *animal* nature'. But no one who reflects on the evils of our contemporary society will fail to realize the nature of the forces with which Paul was contending in seeking to bring the Gentile world of his day into conformity with the Christian demands.

The corruption of the intellectual element in our nature will probably seem less obvious. But that may well be only a reflection on the Church's failure to take this element seriously, to recognize the supremely important contribution which it has to make to religion, and therefore to be sensitive to the subtle forms of perversion to which it is exposed.

The problem with which Paul was coping in seeking to Christianize the intellectual climate of his day can be studied in the second chapter of his first letter to Corinth. The whole chapter will repay exact study. Here we may note some of the contrasts which he draws between what he describes as the two kinds of 'wisdom', the 'psychic' (for which in this context the best translation is perhaps 'natural') and the 'spiritual'. Notice for instance 'the persuasive arguments of (human) intelligence' as against 'the practical demonstration of the power of the Spirit'; 'a faith based on man's power to convince' as against 'a faith based on God's power to convert'; 'the wisdom which is recognized by those who have been initiated (into God's secret)' and 'the wisdom which passes muster with the world, and with the powers that be, who soon become the powers that have been'. The contrast comes to a head in v. 14: 'The man who relies solely on his natural intelligence cannot take the truth which comes from

God. It is mere nonsense to him: he cannot make head or tail of it. For it takes a different kind of discernment, a spiritual one, to understand it.'

Language of this kind was not palatable to many in Paul's day; his reception at Athens indicates that clearly enough. It is no more palatable today. For to many it seems to be a denial of the validity and worth of man's powers of reason, a subordination of that which ought to stand in its own right to some 'supernatural' direction or control. This indeed raises an issue of the greatest importance and difficulty. There is no more urgent problem than that of identifying ways in which the Spirit of God is to be found at work in the ever expanding exercise of man's powers of discovery, research, invention, and distinguishing these from a use of those powers which, because it fails to recognize their true source, can lead only to human self-glorification, and ultimately to self-destruction. The Christian judgement here is balanced on a knife-edge between an abdication which restricts the working of God's Spirit to a sphere of 'religious', even 'ecclesiastical' interests, leaving the whole world of 'secular' knowledge and culture to its own devices, and an illegitimate attempt to claim for religion an all-embracing authority which has long been repudiated.

It was out of such diverse and conflicting material that the new community had to be created. As we read the account of that gradual creation there is no escaping the conclusion that in the minds of those who experienced it one thing was certain. This new unity was not something devised by strategy and organization. It was something *given*. It was the creation of the Spirit of God.

In one of the essays in a now largely forgotten book *The Spirit** edited by Canon Streeter, Dr Anderson Scott asked the question, 'What happened at Pentecost?' His answer is still worth careful study, even though many of his conclusions have passed into the currency of New Testament exegesis.

* Macmillan, 1919.

C

The distinctive outcome of that event was the bringing into
being of something for which from that moment a new name
had to be found, the *koinonia*. It was a new name for a new
fact: the emergence of a new quality of corporate living, a
unity of belief and mutual trust and responsibility which from
this point onwards bound together those who had committed
themselves to Jesus as Lord. The first instance of it occurs
towards the conclusion of the story of Pentecost, in a verse
whose true meaning is obscured in both our Authorized and
Revised translations. 'They persevered steadily in the
Apostles' teaching, and in *the* fellowship, and in the breaking
of bread, and in the prayers' (Acts 2:42). It is not 'the
Apostles' teaching and fellowship'. It is '*the*' fellowship recognized as in itself a distinctive mark of the new life. The word
recurs constantly throughout Paul's letters. There is the verse
(Phil. 2:1) of which a modern translation exactly catches
the significance: 'If Christ makes any appeal to you, if love
carries any sanctions, *if the Spirit has created a real fellowship*,
of which affection and forgivingness are the characteristic
attributes ...'.

Familiarity, a false familiarity contradicted on every hand
by the brute facts of racial strife and class consciousness and
Church divisions, blinds us to the real miracle of this 'breaking down of the middle wall of partition' between Jew and
Gentile – and to its cost. Those who live in areas of acute
colour prejudice or irreconcilable religious apartheid know
well that nothing less than the supernatural power of God's
Spirit can break that bitter entail of human fear and hatred
and blindness. They know also that it happens. And when
they see it happen they can appreciate the fact that only a
miracle of grace can effect such a revolution. Professor J. A.
Findlay once suggested that in the parable of the Pharisee
and the Publican, the Pharisee was probably repeating the
familiar Jewish prayer: 'God, I thank thee that I was born
not a Gentile, but a Jew: not a slave, but a free man: not a

woman, but a man.' And he went on, 'When Paul wrote,
"In Christ there is neither Jew nor Greek, there is neither
slave nor free, there is neither male nor female" he was
deliberately contradicting, phrase by phrase, the prayer
which he had been taught to say from his earliest years.
Something had happened to a man who can do this.'* It
had; and it was happening all around him among his converts. It has got to happen pretty radically in the world – and
in the Church – today.

That revolution was the first and outstanding feature of
the new fellowship. But of course it did not happen in a
vacuum; this unity was not something 'let down in a sheet
by four corners from heaven'. It was not indeed the product
of strategy and organization. But it did not come into being
without them.

There was the practical task of providing for material
needs. Many of the converts were obviously drawn from the
least privileged classes of society. It is likely enough that, as
with converts today, some of them may have paid for their
conversion by the loss of their jobs, and of family support. In
the very earliest days there was that spontaneous pooling of
resources at Jerusalem to meet immediate need. And Acts
and Paul's letters indicate that he recognized in the planning
of mutual support by different local churches a very practical
means of giving ethical reality to what might otherwise have
remained a general and abstract idea of brotherhood. That
was only one of the means employed for strengthening the
links between these scattered groups, for whom isolation
among a pagan majority must often have presented a grave
temptation to relapse. One of the advantages which the
Mediterranean world enjoyed under the Roman Empire was
a freedom and facility for travel hardly paralleled in European history until the nineteenth century. The Christian

* Quoted in Fison, *The Blessing of the Holy Spirit* (Longmans, 1950),
p. 119.

messengers were constantly on the roads and crossing the sea, carrying letters from Paul to one church or another, bringing greetings and news, reporting a critical situation which called for urgent action, building up the sense of belonging to 'the body of Christ'.

That meant something which went much deeper. Dr Scott calls attention to one function of the *koinonia*, which he describes as 'the organ of insight'. No one can read Paul's letters without noting the constant emphasis which he lays upon the necessity for growth in the *understanding* of the new faith which his friends now profess. He prays that the Church in Philippi 'may more and more abound in insight and all manner of perception' (Phil. 1:9). The letter to Ephesus contains a similar prayer that 'being rooted and grounded in love they may be able to comprehend, with all their fellow-Christians, what is the breadth and length and height and depth' (Eph. 3:18). True he distinguishes, as we have already noted, this 'spiritual' knowledge from the mere intellectualism of an already somewhat decadent culture. But he is emphatic that there *is* a Christian wisdom, a Christian *gnosis*, the attainment of which calls for a real exercise of the mind in response to the divine revelation.

It is thus that he comes, at the end of that chapter (1 Cor. 2) in which he contrasts the two wisdoms, to those astonishing concluding words, 'We have the mind of Christ'. That is the goal which he sets before his churches as the means by which their corporate life is to be directed and shaped. They will be constantly facing problems of faith and practice, problems of adjusting themselves to living as Christians in a world in which that demand will be challenged and contradicted by the standards and conventions of their neighbours. And they are to try to look at them through the eyes of Christ, so that gradually there will grow up among them a common ethos, a common standard of reference which reflects the mind of their Master.

In this slow, and often painfully difficult, process of growth the Spirit is the guiding force. He speaks of 'being led by the Spirit'; he tells men 'to walk by the Spirit'; he drives the point home, 'If we claim that we are living in the Spirit, let us behave as though we were' (Gal. 5:25). And as a practical illustration of what that implied we may take one of the most famous episodes in Acts, the story of the Council at Jerusalem (Acts 15).

It was the first major crisis of the new Church. Paul and his friends had embarked upon their Gentile mission. That in itself had aroused opposition from the orthodox Jewish section in Palestine. They had determined that, even if it was impossible to stop Paul letting these outsiders into the Church, they would see to it that he didn't go any further and let them in on easy terms. They should at least accept circumcision. (And it is worth asking ourselves honestly what are the equivalents of this demand in some contemporary negotiations between divided churches.) Paul was equally determined on the other side. His own personal experience in conversion, and what he had seen of the power of Christ's Spirit at work in the lives of his Gentile converts, had settled one question for ever in his own mind. Men came to grace *not* by adherence to the 'works of the Law', by observing the traditional external regulations, but by an act of faith, of trust, in which they committed themselves to Christ. To go back on this, and allow the imposition of the demand for circumcision, would simply be to surrender his own deepest convictions, and to deny the evidence which he had seen with his own eyes of God's power at work in men's lives. It was going to be a head-on collision of principle.

When the Council met there was tremendous argument. And then Paul found a perhaps unexpectedly stout ally in Peter.

Men and brothers, you know that from the earliest days God chose me as one of those from whose lips the Gentiles should hear the Word, and should believe it. Moreover God, who knows men's hearts, has plainly shown that this is so; for when he had cleansed their hearts through their faith, he gave Holy Spirit to the Gentiles exactly as he did to us. Why then must you now strain God's patience by trying to put on the shoulders of those disciples a burden which we and our fathers have always found intolerable? Surely the truth is that it is by the grace of the Lord Jesus that we are saved, through faith, just as they are.

That reduced everybody to silence – as well it might. Then Paul and Barnabas had their chance to tell the assembled company what they had actually seen God doing in this miracle of reconciliation. (Those of us who have listened to Bishops from South India telling a similar story know well what it feels like.)

Finally, James summed up: a compromise solution, yes; but very definitely conceding the main point in Paul's favour. Gentiles did not have to become Jews before they could become Christians. (Again a little reflection on the contemporary situation in reunion discussions will do us no harm.)

And then they wrote their report and an encyclical letter. And it concluded with these words: 'For it has seemed right to the Holy Spirit and to us to lay no further burden upon you beyond that which is absolutely essential.'

'The Holy Spirit and we have come to the conclusion ...' When men can write like that, it can only mean one of two things. Either they are being guilty of an arrogant self-deception by which they can persuade themselves that God must want what they want; or they have experienced what, from time to time, thank God, men do experience in the councils of the Church. They start in rival camps, each sincerely convinced that at no cost must the principles for which they stand be surrendered. And then, because they are honest men, genuinely seeking to know and follow God's will, and humble enough to believe that it may be something different from what they can see of it, they find that something happens. A wisdom not their own takes hold of their respective convictions and shapes out of them something different from either set, and better than either. And they record the decision which has been given them: and they put first the name of the person who has really been the Chairman.

There remains one final aspect of the Spirit's working in the Christian community as we see it depicted in Acts. And it is perhaps the most significant of all. Here again the clue is given us in a passage in the Fourth Gospel which must surely reflect an impression driven home by long experience of surprising, even disconcerting, happenings. 'The wind' ('spirit': in the Greek, and still more in the Hebrew, the two words are barely distinguishable) 'blows where it wills. You can hear the sound of it: but you cannot tell where it comes from, or where it is going. So is everyone in whom the Spirit is the source of life' (John 3:8).

That is what one man had learnt from watching the Spirit at work. Unpredictability. You can't tie the Spirit down. You can't dictate the terms on which it shall work. You can't tell it when to blow, and when to stop. You can't regulate the direction or the force to suit your own plans and preferences.

They had had ample proof of this. At Pentecost they had encountered that 'rushing mighty wind' of the Spirit; and it had swept them away from their moorings as a harmless if somewhat non-conforming sect of the Jewish Church, into the uncharted seas of the Christian mission. Having done that it had taken charge, and kept directing the course, however unexpectedly. As the Church in Antioch 'worshipped and fasted', the fresh direction came. 'Set apart for me Barnabas and Saul. There is special work for which I have chosen them' (Acts 13:2). That was the beginning of the Gentile mission. At times there was a demonstration of stern and irresistible control. 'And now here I am,' says Paul, as he says goodbye to his friends at Miletus, 'compelled by the

Spirit to go to Jerusalem. What will happen to me there I do not know. But in every city the Spirit warns me that imprisonment and persecution await me' (Acts 20:22).

Now and again the action was even more disconcerting, for the Spirit showed no respect for Church rules and regulations. Peter's brave stand at the Council was doubtless the result, in no small measure, of that surprising episode in the case of Cornelius and his friends, when in defiance of the normal order of things the Spirit had anticipated baptism and confirmation, and it was only left for Peter to recognize that, as with the Jewish Sabbath, Church rules were made for men, and not men for Church rules (Acts 10).

CHAPTER 5

The Spirit in the Experience of the Individual

THE best description of the Church in the New Testament is to be found in a phrase which was not, strictly speaking, coined for that purpose: 'A fellowship of Holy Spirit', the kind of community life which is inspired by God's Spirit, the kind of human relationships which become possible when God's Spirit is given the chance to shape them. This unquestionably is the ideal which Paul, and not Paul only, holds before his friends as the experience which they are meant to share, which indeed they are already in some measure sharing.

That was the reason why our detailed study of the work of the Spirit had to begin, in the preceding chapter, with the consideration of its effects at the corporate level. And that this is the right starting point is confirmed by the whole trend of contemporary New Testament scholarship, which with growing unanimity sees not only in the life of the early Church, but in the purpose and mission of its founder, not so much a process of individual conversion and salvation, as the inauguration of a new chosen people, the new Israel, which will at long last fulfil the destiny, so often rejected by the old, the universal mission through which 'the glory of the Lord shall be revealed, and all flesh shall see it together'.

From the beginning of Acts that is where the emphasis falls: those periodical notes in the early chapters which give actual figures for the little group at Jerusalem, and record the addition from time to time of a significant number of new converts, all point in the same direction. It may sound rather like counting heads; but the operative words are always 'there were added to the Church', or some equivalent phrase.

That indeed was the experience of those involved; that was what it felt like. They found themselves taken into, welcomed by, incorporated in a steadily growing family of believers. The new life of which they became conscious was not something primarily dependent on their own efforts; it was, so to speak, a new atmosphere which they found themselves breathing in the new environment into which they had entered.

But it was of course, as it always is, true that the community was a community of persons, of individuals. The quality of its influence was the quality of their personal life and faith. The Spirit was indeed the source of their unity, that most precious of all possessions which it was worth any effort to preserve. But the gift of the Spirit was not an undifferentiated endowment, a mass-produced enthusiasm, or a stock-size 'religious experience'. The Spirit was given to each individual as the means by which he should develop particular capacities and insights as his contribution to the common good (1 Cor. 12:7). (That is undoubtedly the meaning of the concluding words which is obscured by the A.V. and R.V. rendering, 'to profit withal'.) Clearly therefore we must go on to examine in more detail the ways in which men found the Spirit at work in their own personal experience.

It is a formidable task to attempt in one short chapter. To deal with it thoroughly might easily involve us in that kind of Biblical paper-chase beloved of an earlier generation but less congenial to our own. Our method of approach must be a more general one, which, while it may well fail to do justice to some aspects of the evidence, may perhaps serve to bring out the most significant notes which constantly make themselves heard throughout Paul's letters. Of some of them we have already had hints in the two preceding chapters.

There is the note of liberation. It is impossible to miss the impression which recurs in one form or another that these men and women have shared an experience for which passing from darkness into light, from slavery into freedom, from death into life is the only adequate description. 'Where the Spirit of the Lord is, there is liberty' (2 Cor. 3:17). It is of course in a particular context, in which he is dealing with the new understanding of God's revelation in the Old Testament which has come through Jesus, that the phrase occurs. But it might well stand as the signature-tune for a dozen other passages. We may look at one or two.

Consider the impassioned plea of Galatians 3–5. Such a suggestion may well be doubtfully attractive to those whose acquaintance with that particular letter suggests only an ineffectual struggle with some of the most crabbed Rabbinic argument that even Paul ever indulged in. But when one gets below the surface there is no mistaking the intensity of his feeling that he is at grips with an issue which is a matter of life and death.

You daft people of Galatia! who has put a spell on you, you who saw Jesus, the crucified Messiah, set before your eyes so plainly? There is just one question to which I must have an answer. Did you receive the Spirit of God because you were trying to keep the Law, or because you had believed the message of the Gospel? Have you taken leave of your senses? You began your Christian life 'in the Spirit'. Are you going to try to complete it 'in the flesh'? Has all your painful experience [of the cost of becoming Christians] been just waste – if you are thus going to make it just waste? Think! God has poured out his Spirit on you: he has given you all that evidence of the powers which the Spirit can release. Now did he do that because you were being good orthodox law-keepers, or because you had learnt the lesson of faith? (Gal. 3:1–5).

It was for freedom that Christ set you free. Dig in your heels then, and don't be dragged back under the yoke of slavery! (Gal. 5:1).

Clearly something of desperate spiritual importance is at stake. What Paul is wrestling with here is a situation in which a group of Christians *had* seen the light, had broken loose, and were now in danger of relapsing into the old subservience to tradition and convention. It is the crucial issue of getting religion wrong side up or right side up, the difference between trying to 'establish our own righteousness', and trusting in the forgiving mercy of God. And that, as we saw in an earlier chapter, is not a problem which was solved once for all when the Christian Church broke loose from Judaism. It dogs religion in every age.

I can indeed understand those who would protest that in these lax go-as-you-please days a bit of strict 'law-keeping' would be no bad thing for many Christians. But surely the issue goes deeper than that. Why is a good deal of our Church life mediocre, average, tepid, uncommitted? Is it not in part at least just because we are still enslaved by this mistaken idea that all we have to do is to set a standard, so that we can feel that we are keeping somewhere near the mark? And because we have set our aim no higher, because *we* have set our aim, instead of letting the Spirit of God set *his* aim for us, we find our spiritual life, individually and corporately, subjugated to the downward pull of 'safety first'. When we are confronted with a demand for a real experiment, some venture in inter-church cooperation, some appeal for rash and sacrificial giving, we are held back by an inhibition which makes it impossible to respond. 'The glorious liberty of the sons of God' is not a phrase which commonly commends itself to the Church, whether at parochial or at Convocation level.

This discovery of freedom is not a mere emotional experience. To think of it and to treat it as such is indeed a constantly recurring danger. That is why throughout the New Testament there runs the recurrent emphasis on the fact that men are only set free when their eyes are opened to the *truth*. It is of course in the Fourth Gospel that we find this note most clearly struck. 'You shall know the truth, and the truth shall make you free' (John 8:32). 'I will ask the Father, and he will give you another to stand by you, even the Spirit of truth' (14:16). 'When that other comes, the Spirit of truth, he will guide you into all the truth' (16:13). 'For this was I born, and for this I have come into the world, that I should bear witness to the truth. Everyone who belongs to the truth listens to my voice' (18:37).

Whatever view we take of the extent to which the discourses in the Fourth Gospel record the actual sayings of Jesus, this at least is surely clear. The writer has watched, over the years, the Spirit taking the things that belong to Christ and making their meaning clear to his Church. And one of the things which has indeed become clear, as something substantiated over and over again in the lives of ordinary people, is this fact: that it is by knowing the truth that men are set free.

In saying this he is only summing up the experience which is reflected in Acts and Paul's letters. Throughout the story, alongside the sense of liberation, there runs the parallel sense of direction, illumination, growth in insight.

It operated, as we can see, in many different forms and at different levels. There was the clear sense of 'guidance', almost of what one might call 'intervention', which appears in that little story of Paul and his friends on their travels through the provinces of Asia Minor (Acts 16:6 ff.). And it is important to note the form in which that guidance came. It was not that they had abdicated from the use of natural talents of foresight and planning. On the contrary; they had got a clear picture of what they were aiming at, and when, on the first occasion, that ended in a full-stop, they put their minds to it again. The same thing happened a second time. And it was only as they reflected upon the curious sense which they had had on both occasions, that there was another directing power at work all the time, that the true significance of the events became clear.

One point emerges here of cardinal importance. There have been in our time movements which have rightly sought to emphasize and develop this sense of guidance which was

familiar enough to Christians of an earlier generation. That
they have done a valuable piece of work thereby no one
would deny. But at times they have failed rather egregiously
at two points. They have tended, unintentionally maybe, to
depreciate the natural endowment of intelligence and foresight, and therefore to weaken instead of strengthen the sense
of responsibility for the use of those powers. The gift of
the Spirit is never represented in the New Testament as a
substitute for the exercise of rational judgement. It is, we are
told, a safeguard against 'being anxious', against that fretful
debilitating temper which springs from relying *only* upon our
own intelligence and ability, and forgetting that there is any
such thing as 'the wisdom which is from above'.

More serious still has been the emphasis upon guidance as
a momentary instantaneous intervention, a guarantee as one
might say of an immediate supply of hot water upon the
turning of the tap. This is unfortunate for two reasons. It can
result at times in what is a reduction of the practice to a mere
triviality, which seeks to justify itself by turning coincidence
into divine response. But much more serious is the fact that it
tends to obscure the truth that seeking the guidance of God is
not a matter of occasional spasmodic recourse to an oracle,
but a slow process of orientation and training of the spiritual
faculty. 'As many as are *led* by the Spirit of God ...'; and to
be led one must walk and go on walking.

There are, of course, certain occasions, the making of really
big decisions, the facing of acutely difficult choices, in which
we feel that we do need, and have a right to ask for, the
direction of God's wisdom on this particular immediate issue.
And we do well to ask for it. We cannot assume that we shall
always receive it on the spot, at least in a form in which we
recognize it as such. A great deal of such guidance is only
discoverable *ex post facto*, even years later.

But there are far more days in our lives when no such
critical situation occurs; and it is in these routine periods that

we can learn to cultivate the kind of spiritual receptivity which will stand us in good stead, both in the ordinary conduct of life and when the major decisions present themselves. We can make a regular practice of training ourselves in what we may call sensitiveness to the will of God, not an expectancy of sudden illumination, but a growing capacity to perceive opportunities, possibilities, indications of Christ-like action. Simply to look ahead for a day or a week, with the engagement book in hand if our work is of that kind, and try to sense the situations which are likely to call for some special exercise of honesty, patience, or courage, is an excellent way of going into training. We shall find at times, to our dismay *and* to our encouragement, that we are by this means led into situations which we should not have chosen, but which do present openings for a considerable venture of faith, a response to the Spirit. That is the way in which, for some at least, guidance seems to come much more surely.

It is here that we can see the true meaning of Paul's constantly repeated hope and prayer for *growth* in this capacity, 'that your love may increase more and more in knowledge and every kind of sensitive understanding' (Phil. 1:9), 'that God will give you the Spirit of wisdom by which his secrets are revealed, as you grow in the knowledge of him' (Eph. 1:17).

At the practical level one can see this process at work in those chapters (5–8) in the first letter to Corinth, in which he deals point by point with a series of difficult moral problems which have been reported to him. They are the kind of problem which arises in a community which is slowly and painfully trying to grow up into Christian standards of conduct, and is finding it no easy matter to know how that demand can be met in face of the current ethical habits of the surrounding society.

At a deeper level this growth in spiritual insight takes us into the very heart of Christian faith. 'No man can say, Jesus

is Lord, except through the insight which the Spirit gives'
(1 Cor. 12: 3). There indeed is a saying which, when we stop to
think about it, brings home with painful sharpness the dull
monotony with which we habitually repeat these tremendous
words. For to those who first used them, to acknowledge Jesus
as Lord was a step which might involve drastic consequences.
In our own day we can see the same thing in more than one
country in which the secular power has decided that it will
brook no rival to its lordship. But it comes nearer home than
that. To call Jesus Lord is a mere empty phrase unless it
means *seeing* him as Lord and taking the consequences of
accepting him as such. And not so many days go by in the
life of many members of the Church on which some issue
does not arise which challenges the sincerity of that acceptance.

A third key-word is 'power'. 'God who has given you all
that evidence of the powers which the Spirit can release'
(Gal. 3:5). Our Bibles usually translate it 'mighty works' or
'miracles', and that is probably the natural association which
the word raises in our minds. That is of course one of the
meanings which the word bears in the New Testament context: and unquestionably Jesus himself had claimed that his
own power to deal with many forms of nervous and psycho-
somatic illness was evidence of the irruption of a new force
into human life. 'You say that I cast out demons because I
am in league with their chief. Could be: though it makes it
awkward for your own professional exorcists, doesn't it? But
there is another possible explanation. If I by the finger of
God' (Matthew reads 'Spirit' for 'finger') 'cast out these
demons, then do you see what it means? The Reign of God
has come upon you unawares' (Luke 11:14–20).

What is more, there is a hint, in that little fragment of
post-Resurrection conversation preserved in the opening
verses of Acts, that he had given them a clear indication that
they might expect to share in that same gift. He had said that

they were going to receive 'a baptism in Holy Spirit' in a few days; and he had made it clear what that would imply. 'You shall receive power' (and *dunamis* is strangely like 'dynamite') 'when the Holy Spirit has taken hold of you' (Acts 1:8). They had. But they had found, as they might have expected if they had learnt the lesson which throughout his ministry he had been continually trying to teach them, that the true nature of this power was not to be discerned in its more spectacular manifestations. It was, if I remember rightly, Dr Maltby who remarked that on a true reading of the purpose of the Lord's ministry the conversion of Zaccheus was a greater 'miracle', a greater demonstration of power, than the feeding of the five thousand.

That is a truth which could be demonstrated many times over from the evidence of Paul's letters. Here are one or two passages which bring out clearly what it had meant to him to know this power of the Spirit at work in his own ministry.

We call to mind, my brothers, what happened when the love of God called you at your conversion. We brought the Gospel to you: but it was not just a matter of preaching. There was a power at work, the power of the Holy Spirit, and it showed its effects. You know how we lived among you: and you remember how you set yourselves to follow our example. It meant sharp persecution. But the Holy Spirit enabled you to face it with joy (1 Thess. 1:4–6).

And the same note recurs in another passage in which Paul reveals for a moment his very human weaknesses.

I was feeling ill when I came to visit you. Frankly, I was frightened: I had rather lost my nerve. When I spoke and preached to you there was no spell-binding eloquence about it: but none the less it gave the Spirit the chance to show his power. Clearly you were meant to put your trust not in a clever presentation by a man, but in the power of God (1 Cor. 2:3–5).

It was a lesson which some of his converts did not find it easy to learn. That chapter (12) in the first letter to Corinth in which he deals at length with the question of 'spiritual gifts' brings out clearly enough the difficulty which he had in training that particular Church in a true sense of proportion. Within the Church of England at any rate there may be little danger of men being misled by outbreaks in the congregation of 'ecstatic speech and prophecy'. But the underlying danger is still present. There is a tendency, and all the more perhaps at a time when to many religion seems to have lost some of its freshness, to cry for some unusual, even spectacular, exhibition of power; it may be in preaching, it may be in that more subtle and dangerous realm of 'personality'. The true test still remains the same. The effective presence of the Spirit is known, as it has always been, by the fact that men's lives are being changed, that they are being lifted out of conventional goodness, or out of downright evil, by an influence which they know is *not* that of any human attraction or persuasion.

And so we come to the point at which the basic characteristic of the Spirit's working is laid bare.

Dr Barrett, in the book to which I have already referred, notes the fact that *pneuma* (Spirit) is not the only word to which surprisingly few references are made in the Gospels. *Hagios* (Holy) is another. And Canon Fison in his book *The Blessing of the Holy Spirit** takes up the point and develops it. By the time the ministry of Jesus began, 'holiness' which figures as one of the dominant notes of the Old Testament had, if we may use a homely phrase, gone sour. The great prophets of the eighth century had stamped it with that truly ethical quality which had characterized their religious revival. But once the first flush of the post-exilic reforming enthusiasm had waned, religion had settled down into a terrible stalemate of legalism and ceremonialism. Holiness had become a matter of ritual purity, of separation from any outside contact which might defile, of strict observance of rules. It had lost the fire of moral passion for righteousness. It

* Longmans, 1950.

had become the kind of temper which could criticize Jesus for healing on the Sabbath Day. It had become a pietistic, if not an ecclesiastical, virtue. If Jesus was concerned to salvage and vindicate the true conception of the Spirit, he was equally concerned to do the same for 'holy'. 'The conclusion', writes Canon Fison, 'is clear: *hagios*, like *pneuma*, is a dangerous word and needs reinterpreting before it can be safely used.' It is not only of the first century that this could be said.

The reinterpretation had been given in the life and character of Jesus. Indeed it had been nothing less than a moral revolution. A righteousness had been demonstrated which did indeed 'exceed the righteousness of Scribes and Pharisees' because it started from quite a different premiss. Its inspiration was the infinite love of God which does not ask that men shall become 'holy' before they can be loved, but takes them as they are and loves them into holiness. It had been carried through in face of misrepresentation and opposition to the bitter end. It had been in the acceptance of dereliction on the Cross that the meaning, and the cost, of true holiness had been revealed.

And because in this 'Jesus had been glorified', the true character and power of the Spirit could now be known; and the fruit of them could now begin to grow.

'The fruit of the Spirit is love, joy, peace, patience, kindliness, generosity, trustworthiness, gentleness, self-control' (Gal. 5:22). There is no mistaking the original from which that picture is drawn. And it was in the slow cultivation of that fruit, 'Paul sowing, Apollos watering, but God giving the increase', that the full work of the Spirit was seen.

Famous and well-loved passages like this one tend only too easily to become staled and blunted by familiarity. It calls for constant re-examination to recover the depth of their meaning.

It is the 'fruit' of the Spirit, as contrasted with the 'works' of the flesh. And the contrast is significant. 'Works' are something that we do; 'fruit' is something which grows. Once again we are reminded of that 'great divide' which runs through all Paul's teaching, the contrast between reliance upon our unaided human powers, which so often only produces results which are a lamentable contradiction of what we are aiming at, and trusting in the power of God, giving his Spirit the opportunity to cultivate his fruit. We might paraphrase the opening words: 'These are the kind of qualities that you may expect to see beginning to grow in a man's life, when the Spirit is given the chance to operate.'

When we turn to look at the actual list, one thing becomes immediately apparent. With possibly one exception, the qualities included are such as only show themselves in their true light when seen in terms of human relationships. What we have here is, so to speak, the content of 'a fellowship of Holy Spirit'. Here is the charter for the citizens of a community which is seeking to make its social relationships expressive of the spirit of Christ. Here indeed is one more decisive proof that the Christian life can never be understood or realized if it is thought of as an individual aim or achievement.

Is what has just been written mere pious verbiage? Take these qualities each in turn, and set them against the background of daily life: home, school, shop, factory, government department. Have they any real relevance to the demands which arise in these, and a hundred other spheres, every day of the week? We shall have to return in a later chapter to the contribution which a Christian interpretation of life ought to be making in these spheres. For the moment it may be sufficient to remind ourselves that if the Parables of the Gospel are any guide, it is precisely from what men do, or do not do, in the conduct of their affairs in this 'secular' world that Jesus drew his analogies in interpreting his central message of 'the Reign of God'. And as an exercise in personal self-examination, we can look at a week's work in whatever job we happen to be employed, and ask what difference it would make to the running of it, if it were more widely recognized that it is upon the exercise of such qualities as these that the happiness, reliability, and efficiency of men's daily work largely depend.

There remains one further question to be asked, the crucial one. How do all these experiences of liberation, illumination, power, growth in Christian character come? How do we 'give the Spirit the chance to operate' in our lives?

The answer of the New Testament is familiar to the point of exasperation! It is an answer in two words: Faith and Prayer. But before we throw in our hand at being fobbed off again with the demands which have defeated us so often, it is worth looking rather more carefully at what the New Testament writers – for with minor differences they all agree – mean by these two words.

There is a famous passage (Rom. 10:13) in which Paul sets out some of the essential stages by which faith is reached. (And remember that 'faith' or 'belief' can nearly always be translated equally well as 'trust'). 'Everyone who calls upon the name of the Lord shall be saved.' (Yes, it's all very well to say things like that, but ...) How can men call on a God in whom they have never believed, to whom they can't pin their faith? And how can men believe in a God of whom they have never heard (at least in terms of which they could make any sense)? And how can they hear unless someone really makes it plain to them?

We can see clearly enough some of the essential steps by which men come to faith. There must be the clear presentation of what it is that they are asked to accept, to believe, to trust. Faith is not something that we produce out of our own inside; it is not something that we construct by our own imagination; it is a response to something which is set forth as truth. That response is not a forced response, under the pressure of emotional stimulus. There must be a 'hearing' of the truth, a deliberate concentration of attention upon its content, an intelligent attempt to understand and weigh its claim. Then and only then can the final step be taken, the appropriation of the truth, the making it one's own. And that act of appropriation is one in which all the faculties are involved, desire and choice and commitment completing the work of understanding.

It is indeed this final step which is the hardest to take. It is quite easy to be interested in Christianity: lots of people are nowadays. And it is quite interesting to discuss it and argue about it: lots of people do. It is desperately hard to bring oneself to the point of saying, 'Yes, I see. I can't sit on the fence any longer. I'll try it: here goes!', and to keep on saying that as each stage of the experiment opens up new situations, intellectual and moral, in which the same plunge has got to be taken again, into what looks like rather deeper water.

Is it so difficult, in the light of what we have seen so far, to see what committing one's life to the Spirit really means?

But everything in these last few paragraphs could be entirely misleading if it conveyed, as it might, that this whole approach to faith was something which *we* had to make in order to receive the Spirit. We follow this road and find the Spirit waiting at the end to greet us. Nothing could be a more complete misrepresentation of the New Testament view.

In his lecture on the Holy Spirit in *Christian Belief* Dr Vidler makes this extremely important comment:

It is highly significant, and easily overlooked, that in the New Testament Christians do not *pray for* the coming of the Spirit. They *live in* the Spirit; it is he who enables them to pray. They have not to call down an absent Spirit, but only to recall that they have been received once for all into a relationship with God, which means that they permanently have the Spirit in the depths of their being, if not on the surface of their consciousness. Prayers for the coming of the Spirit which are often used by Christians now, can no doubt be interpreted consistently with this: but they are liable to mislead. It is the Collect for Whitsunday in the Book of Common Prayer which strikes the right note.

In verification of this we need only turn to that great passage in Romans 8:12–27, the *locus classicus* for the work of the Holy Spirit in the human soul. 'We know that up to this moment all created life groans in a kind of universal travail. Not only that: we who already have a foretaste [an instalment] of the Spirit, we too share this anguish, as we wait for the full realization of our sonship, which means the redemption of this life in the body' (vv. 22, 24). 'So too the Spirit comes to the rescue of our weakness [the Greek verb might be used for the rescue of a drowning man]. For by ourselves we don't know what we should rightly pray for. But the Spirit itself intercedes for us with sighs which can find no utterance in words. And he who knows the secrets of our hearts knows also what is the intention of those prayers which the Spirit offers to God for us' (vv. 26, 27).

That may take us out of our depth. We had not realized that that was what was happening when we try to pray. But there are phrases here which strike a chord of response. That sense of frustrated longing – how are we to pray for a world which has so desperately lost its way, of which we know so little, in which we can apparently do so little? And every now and again – not more perhaps for many of us – the sudden realization, when we have nearly been down for the third time, that there *is* a power not our own at work which is prompting the prayers, however futile they seem, and which is being heard.

'Thou wouldst not seek, unless thou hadst already found', wrote Pascal in a famous phrase. Would he have been even nearer the truth if he had written 'unless thou hadst already *been* found'?

CHAPTER 6

Who is the Spirit?

WRITING these last three chapters was a rather tantalizing business. I have a hope that it may have been the same reading them. We have been taking evidence from various parts of the New Testament, and taking it somewhat at its face value, trying to build up a picture of the experience which the writers describe as 'the coming of the Holy Spirit', and of the effects of that experience in the life of the community and of individual souls. And all the time we appear to have been dodging the really essential question: Who – or what – *is* this Holy Spirit? What have they to say about that?

May I remind you that this was to be a 'non-theological' book. I made it plain in the Introduction that that was a phrase which would have to be taken with a grain of salt. But I did also suggest that writers who have to use technical theological language – and of course there is no escaping it – should at least try to prepare the way for the use of such terms by presenting a picture of some human situation which would be recognizable by the reader as at least in some measure familiar ('Oh! Yes, I see what this man is driving at: I've been there myself'). That is what these last three chapters have been attempting to do; and I can only hope that as a result we have reached the point at which we feel that this 'influence' or 'power' (to give it no more precise definition) is something which we ourselves have in some measure experienced or would like to experience, and are therefore anxious to discover more exactly its nature and source.

It might be thought, in view of the frequency of the references, at any rate in Acts and Epistles, that there would be little difficulty in answering this basic question. Surely, when the Spirit has bulked so largely in their lives, the writers will have left us in no doubt on the main point. But it is a commonplace of theological study that this is not the case.

Strictly speaking, the New Testament hardly provides us with a coherent worked-out presentation of any of the affirmations of faith which later took shape in the Creeds. Nor is that really a matter for surprise when we consider the circumstances in which the books were written, or the stage of theological development which they represent. Perhaps an analogy may serve to illustrate the point. Excavation is in process on an important archaeological site. Gangs of men are at work, under the supervision of a handful of experts, digging out the main lines of the building. All the time finds are being unearthed: bones, tiles, pottery, implements. Many of them are mere bits and pieces which have to be carefully collected, to be sorted and put together later on. As the work goes on, there is no time to do more than make notes, a provisional assessment of the day's bag. The proper identification and classification of the finds, still more the working out of a comprehensive account of the particular phase of civilization which they represent, will have to wait until there is time for comparison, cross-reference, reflection, and considered judgement. Actually, so far as the doctrine of the Holy Spirit is concerned, that time never came during the New Testament period. In a curious way it never does seem to have come in the history of theological thought.

In the face of such a situation it is perhaps permissible, and indeed the most useful method of approach, to take the collection of fragmentary evidence as it presents itself in the original documents, and see what we can do ourselves to piece it together and make something like a reconstruction.

For the moment we shall leave on one side the evidence available from the first three Gospels, though we shall come back to take that into account later on. And we shall ask the reader to take certain selected passages from Paul's letters and the Fourth Gospel, and make a careful study of them for himself. The passages are Rom. 8:1–27 (especially 8–11); 2 Cor. 3:12–18 (especially 16–18), 13:13 (see also Eph. 2:18, 3:14–17); John 14:15–26, 15:26, 16:5–15.

Take certain phrases from these passages and just put them down side by side. 'If the Spirit of God dwells in you', 'if a man does not possess the Spirit of Christ', 'if Christ is in you', 'if the Spirit of him who raised Jesus from the dead dwells in you', 'now the Lord is the Spirit', 'where the Spirit of the Lord is', 'the Grace of the Lord Jesus Christ, and the love of God, and the fellowship of the Holy Spirit be with you', 'I will ask the Father, and he will send you another to stand by you … even the Spirit of truth', 'I will not leave you orphaned, I will come to you', 'if a man loves me he will keep my word, and my Father will love him, and we will come to him', 'but the stand-by, the Holy Spirit, whom the Father will send in my name', 'when the stand-by comes, whom I will send to you from the Father'.

Take these phrases: study them in their contexts, and see what you can make of the jig-saw. Is it possible to make out of them a coherent statement of how the men who wrote them conceived of the relation of Father, Son, and Spirit? Is it possible even to make two such statements, for Paul and John respectively?

It might well seem as though the best we could do would be to conclude that the New Testament hesitates between three alternative views: (1) The Spirit is God, just God. His activity is the power of God impinging directly upon the souls of men; (2) The Spirit is the *alter ego* of Jesus. His activity is the inspiration of Jesus, risen and glorified; (3) There are three recognizably distinct sources of divine action and inspiration, Father, Son, Spirit.

Clearly no one of these taken in isolation can represent the full New Testament view; equally clearly, to leave them standing side by side is simply to accept contradiction without any attempt to resolve it. We must examine them more closely, trying to identify the experience on which each statement depends; we must compare one with another, and see whether we can construct some coherent scheme which will include the truth for which each of them separately appears to stand. Let us try to do it from the point of view of those who recorded the evidence.

Note first that that is what they were doing. The doctrine of the Trinity – for that is of course what we now have to consider – was not a doctrine arrived at by abstract speculation about the nature of God. It was the result of an attempt to formulate, in so far as it is possible for human language to do that, truths which men were convinced had come home to them as they reflected on facts of experience. It was, one may say, a doctrine arrived at empirically, as the result of observation.

These men were devout and convinced monotheists. For them as for their fathers, since Israel became a covenant nation, there was one God, 'beside whom there is none other'. But that God had made himself known to their nation through the agency of his 'Spirit'. That had shown itself through the calling and endowment of particular men for special tasks: kings, national heroes, above all prophets. Such endowment had been selective and, as it were, intermittent. The Spirit could come upon an individual, and it could leave him again. But all along they had sensed that this was only a partial demonstration of the Spirit's nature and power. The greatest of their national leaders had expressed the passionate wish that 'all the Lord's people were prophets, and that the Lord would put his spirit upon them!' (Num. 11:29). They had cherished the hope that there would come a day when God would 'pour out his Spirit upon all flesh: your sons and your daughters shall share the prophetic inspiration: your young men shall see visions and your old men shall dream dreams: and even upon slaves and slave-girls in those days will I pour out my Spirit, saith the Lord' (Joel 2:28, 29). And alongside this they had cherished another hope: that there would come one in whom this possession by the Spirit of God would be no longer intermittent – 'the Spirit of the Lord shall *rest* upon him' (Isa. 11:2).

Some of them had been eye-witnesses of a life in which, and as the result of which, they believed that these hopes had been fulfilled. They had noted his authority, the unquestioning claim to know the mind and will of God, the claim to exercise powers over the bodies and souls of men which only God could exercise. And they had noted that the message which he preached, and the welcome which he extended, were clearly not confined to any aristocracy of birth or wealth or education or piety. 'The common people listened to him gladly.'

There had been a black moment when that life had ended in apparent disaster and failure. 'This was the man who, we had trusted, was going to redeem Israel' – and now ... And then they had come out on the other side. And that experience of seeing unbelievable victory won out of the jaws of defeat had convinced them once for all that his claim *had* been true. They came forward as men prepared to witness to that faith.

But they found themselves witnessing to something more than that. The Spirit which they had seen in Jesus was now at work in themselves. Now indeed the prophecy of Joel was being fulfilled under their eyes; small shop-keepers and dock-labourers, yes, and slaves, were sharing in this gift.

And there was another discovery, of even greater significance. In the earliest stages the influence of the Spirit had shown itself mainly in the heightening of men's natural powers, physical vigour, intelligence, sometimes artistic ability, or in an access of ecstatic fervour producing 'prophetic' outbursts, such as have persisted even into our own time in 'dervish' groups. In the great eighth-century prophets it had indeed developed on to an infinitely higher plane of moral and spiritual insight. But even so it can be said that throughout the Old Testament period the emphasis on transformation of *character*, as the result of the Spirit's influence, plays but a comparatively small part.

Now something different had happened. Because 'Jesus had been glorified', because men had seen in him the true character of the servant of God, the Spirit's power could be, and was being, released in its true form. Now it becomes possible to see what *Holy* Spirit really meant.

How did they describe and explain what they were finding? In particular, how did they attempt to define the relation between those different elements in their experience, which had, as a matter of experience, come to them successively in time?

Clearly it was the work of God. No other explanation could account for its transforming effects. But it was, if one can so put it, the work of God with a difference, the difference which had come through the radical modification of their conception of God made by the life, death, and resurrection of their Master. The activity of God, through the Spirit, had been raised to a new degree, given a new richness of meaning and content, not indeed added, but now realized for the first time. The Spirit was seen to be the Spirit of Jesus, not only the Spirit as it had been in Jesus, while he was with them, but the Spirit as it was continuing to be in Jesus, still effective, even more widely effective, in their own lives. As we saw, they found it difficult to know whether to think of it as simply the continuation of his power, risen and glorified. It is not easy to be certain, for instance, exactly how Paul would have distinguished between his two great phrases 'life *in Christ*' and 'life *in the Spirit*'. But that there *was* a distinction in their minds is indicated, even were there no other evidence to support it, by that one closing greeting at the end of 2 Corinthians, 'The grace of the Lord Jesus Christ, and the love of

God, and the fellowship of the Holy Spirit'. The very fact
that elsewhere 'the grace of the Lord Jesus Christ' is used as
an adequate salutation makes the one occasion when 'the
fellowship of the Holy Spirit' is added more significant.

Could we summarize the evidence, so far, by saying that
they might have described the Spirit as that aspect of the
being of God, and that mode of God's activity, the full nature
of which is made known, and the full operation of which is
made possible, through the Incarnation, the revelation of God
in the life of Jesus?

Such a statement will, in some minds, give rise to question,
and even call out an immediate repudiation. 'Aspect' and
'mode' are dangerous words, it will be said. They have appeared before in the history of doctrinal debate, and they
have been rejected, and rightly rejected, by the mind of the
Church as misleading and indeed heretical. There is for
orthodox belief one word, and one word only, which may be
regarded as a true and sufficient description. 'Fatherhood',
'Sonship', and 'Spirithood' are not 'aspects' or 'modes' of
the Godhead. They are 'Persons' within the unity of the
Trinity.

No one at all familiar with contemporary religious thought,
especially among young people, is under any illusions as to
the difficulties which this kind of language raises. They have
got to be faced. It is intolerable that the belief which is
affirmed to be the heart of the Christian faith in God should
just be left as a meaningless puzzle, an apparent offence
against rational interpretation. That it is, as the being of
God must always be, a 'mystery' may well be allowed. But
there is all the difference in the world between 'This is high:
I cannot attain unto it', and 'This is nonsense: I can't make
head or tail of it'.

Christianity is a monotheistic religion. It believes in one
God. It believes that there can only be one God, for the good
and sufficient reason, among others, that on no other basis is

the conception of a Uni-verse possible. Whatever the doctrine of three Persons in one God may mean, it does *not* mean tritheism.

What the Christian faith does affirm is that the unity of God is not a bare mathematical unity. It is that, in the sense that unity is the opposite of multiplicity. There is only one God. But it is also an organic unity, the nature of which is, so to speak, that it is not uni-cellular.* It is a unity subsisting in three '*personae*'. The Latin word *persona*, like the Greek words *prosopon* or even *hypostasis*, did not mean either 'person' or 'personality' in the sense in which we commonly use these words, as implying a distinct centre of consciousness. It meant originally the status held, or the function discharged, by an individual in the life of the community; and then, by transference, the person holding that status or discharging that function. The nearest equivalent in current usage is the survival of the phrase 'dramatis personae', the roles in a drama, and so the actors taking those roles. When we try to find an exact English equivalent, it is extraordinarily hard to do so. It is true that the words 'aspect' or 'mode' are inadequate. They imply too much a temporary phase through which the 'person' passes, a partial expression of his full individuality. On the other hand, 'person' is misleading. It suggests too much the idea of 'an individual'. Perhaps the nearest we can get is to say that the nature of God is personal, existing and expressing itself in three eternal characters and activities which together constitute the divine being.

We need to remind ourselves continually that, as I said earlier, the doctrine of the Trinity was a doctrine arrived at empirically. It was the result of taking the evidence of historical experience seriously. Men found themselves compelled to recognize and distinguish three 'moments' in the revelation which had come to them of God's nature and activity.

* Cf. L. Hodgson, *The Doctrine of the Trinity* (Nisbet, 1943).

But the word 'moment' needs to be safeguarded from misunderstanding. It *has* a temporal implication, in the sense
that the revelation came to men in the unfolding of the
sequence of historical events. But that temporal implication
applies only to the giving and acceptance of the revelation,
not to a development within the being of God so revealed.
The Church found itself grappling with this mistaken inference from an early stage. And it had to resist firmly the suggestion implied in some of the early heresies that the Incarnation
implied a temporal enrichment, enlargement, extension of the
being of God, in the crude sense, which one or two of those
heresies came near to asserting, that 'God now had a Son'.
The famous anathemas attached to the Creed of Nicaea make
this plain enough. ('And those who say that there was a time
when the Son did not exist ... these the Church repudiates.')
Similarly the Biblical evidence made it plain that the coming
of the Spirit at Pentecost, or at the Baptism of Jesus, did not
mark the emergence of a new factor or phase in the being of
God. The activity of the Spirit in Creation, and in the religious growth of the Hebrew people ('Who spoke through the
Prophets'), was sufficient safeguard against this second error.
The Church considered, and firmly rejected, what was called
an 'economic' doctrine of the Trinity, the idea that God's
nature adjusts itself, grows new organs, if one may so put it,
to meet new situations and demands. It affirmed, beyond
question, that what we mean by Fatherhood, Sonship, and
Spirithood are all eternally present in the being of God, that
they are the essential characteristics which make God's being
what it is.

Can we translate this into language which, though perhaps
not much easier, is at least a little nearer to our ordinary ways
of thinking? There is, within the being of God, pure Godhead,
God as he is in himself, wholly transcendent. But if this were
all that God is, if he were nothing else, there could be no
going out from himself in creation: he would remain a bare

self-contained and self-sufficient 'Unit'. There is also present within the being of God his Logos, his Word, reason, power of self-communication, the inherent necessity to express himself in act. But this again, by itself, is not sufficient. It is, in itself, only the potentiality, even the necessity, of expression, of communication, but not the action itself. That is the work of the Spirit whose characteristic description is that he 'proceeds', goes out in creation and inspiration, from the Father and the Son.

We have of course, in reaching even this elementary stage of definition, moved far beyond the confines of New Testament evidence. We are already nearer the thought of the fourth than of the first century. If this book aimed at being anything like a serious study of the development of the theology of the Spirit, it would be necessary at this point to carry the more detailed survey which has been given of the thought of the New Testament on to a similar study of the patristic period.

As a matter of fact the result would not be particularly rewarding. For it is a well-established fact that the theological attention of the Church during the first three or four centuries was focused mainly on other aspects of the faith. So far as the doctrine of the Spirit is concerned, the writers for the most part confined themselves to elaborating the evidence provided directly by Scripture. And here it would seem they found themselves hampered by the fact that the New Testament writers had so to speak pre-empted most of the evidence available from such sources as the Wisdom literature, which might have been properly employed in working out a theology of the Spirit, and applied it to the elaboration and enrichment of the doctrine of the Logos. As a result only a few cardinal points received special emphasis. There was a continual insistence on the necessity of preserving the unity of the Godhead against any tendency to distinguish the operation of the three *personae* in such a way as might open the door to the possibility of tritheism. To quote Dr Kelly's recent and most valuable survey of early Christian doctrine: 'The divine action begins from the Father, proceeds through the Son, and is completed in the Holy Spirit: none of the Persons possesses a separate operation of his own, but one identical energy passes through all three.'* This emphasis was of course equally important as a safeguard against the tendency to regard the Spirit as in some way subordinate, a mere agency of, or emanation from, deity. As against this there is a sustained insistence on the 'equality of substance', a mode of expression which, while it reflects the philosophical background of the time, unmistakably asserts the essential truth that the Spirit is indeed God in action.

It is in Augustine's great treatise *De Trinitate* that patristic thought receives its fullest expression. He reaffirms the cardinal points already alluded to, laying the greatest possible emphasis upon the unity and equality of the three Persons. But his most original contribution is to be found in the elaboration of a number of analogies drawn from the structure of the human soul, in which in the triad of being, knowing, and willing he finds 'a vestige of the triune nature of God'. But he himself is the first to admit the inadequacy of human language to find appropriate forms of expression. 'Yet when it is asked what the three are, human utterance is weighed down by a deep poverty of speech. All the same we say three "persons", not because we wish to say it, but that we may not be reduced to silence.'

Is that somewhat pessimistic, if salutary, confession of man's incapacity to express the nature of the divine being the only conclusion to be reached as the result of these centuries of patient thought and argument? I think not. There are two directions at least in which it is possible to recognize the signal contribution made to the thought and life of Christendom by the determined insistence of the Fathers that the true nature of God is to be stated in the Trinitarian formula.

* Kelly, *Early Christian Creeds* (Longmans, 1950), p. 267.

We are familiar with the statement that it was the Christian Church which came to the rescue of the Roman Empire in its decline and salvaged from the wreck of classical culture elements of permanent value which were to form a large part of the basis of European civilization. But it is not always realized that the heart of that operation was to be found in the rethinking and restatement of the tradition of philosophical and scientific thought inherited from Aristotle, which had run into a dead end through certain errors in the original formulation which made it impossible to provide a satisfying explanation of the relation of God to the world of nature.

The question is discussed in detail in Professor Cochrane's brilliant study *Christianity and Classical Culture*,* and in the late Professor R. G. Collingwood's second volume of Philosophical Studies, *An Essay on Metaphysics*.† The really significant point which emerges from both these studies is that it was precisely the formulation of a Trinitarian faith that provided the presuppositions on which the tradition of scientific thinking in Europe has rested for the last fourteen centuries.

For the full statement of the evidence the reader must refer to the works just mentioned. But very briefly stated the argument may be put thus. The 'Catholic Faith' which emerges by the fifth century makes these basic affirmations:

1. There is one God. Here of course the Christian thinkers are in line both with the tradition of Hebrew monotheism and with the philosophical tradition of the Greeks in its protest against prevalent polytheism.

2. This one God is the creator of the world. Here they part company with the Greek line of thought – which had seen in God only the model of perfection which the world seeks to imitate in self-creation – and align themselves with the Hebrew creation myth. The truth of God as creator they

* Clarendon Press, 1940. See chapter x, pp. 361 ff. xi.
† Clarendon Press, 1940. See chapter xxi.

would affirm as the absolute presupposition of a single science of nature.

3. But this very truth of God as creator has implications of great significance for the nature of God. It implies that the unity of his being is a self-differentiating unity. And the recognized word in Greek philosophical thought for such a self-differentiating unity is Logos. It is not difficult to pick up the connexion here with the Prologue of the Fourth Gospel, in which the writer unmistakably recapitulates *and* rewrites the creation story, using language which reflects the phraseology of current Platonism, but adds the distinctively Christian affirmation that this creative Logos had taken human life in the person of Jesus.

4. The nature of the creative act consisted, and consists, in the enduing of created life with movement. Here again the Christian thinkers abandoned the typically Greek line of thought in favour of the Genesis creation myth, in which the Spirit (breath) of God moves upon the face of the waters, and God breathes his Spirit into the man whom he has made.

The second effect of the long struggle to work out the meaning of Trinitarian belief takes us out of abstract thought into the very heart of religious faith. If the doctrine of the Trinity is true, if historically it stands in permanent contradiction of any unitarian or monistic belief, then it is bound to have an effect not only upon our theology but upon the springs of our worship and life.

When we examine these honestly, would it not be true to say that a good deal which passes current as Christian faith and doctrine is *not* really Trinitarian? It could, I believe, not unfairly be characterized under one of two other types.

For some the focus of their faith and worship is God the Father, but often enough conceived less truly as *Father* than as King, Judge, Creator, remote, transcendent, 'the wholly other'. This is not the Christian faith: it is a partially Christianized form of Judaism or Islam.

For others the focus is the person of our Lord, whether thought of primarily in terms of the earthly life depicted in the Gospels, or as the risen and ascended Christ. In one form it is commonly to be found in Liberal Protestantism; in the other in various types of mysticism and pietism, both Catholic and Protestant. But this again is less than the full faith.

Both of these types suffer from two defects. In the first place they both, strange as it may seem, give a 'reduced' value to the truth of the Incarnation. The former fails to give a true value to God *in Christ*: the latter to *God* in Christ. But further they both fail to supply just that element of faith, and its dynamic, from the lack of which so much of our present-day religion suffers. Neither of them adequately represents or conveys the inspiration of God present and active in the world of events, of contemporary life. We shall have to return to this point at some length when we come in the concluding chapters to ask what a Church which really believed in the Spirit would be like. Here and now we register the point that that is just precisely the missing element. We are ignoring the Third Person of the Trinity.

The results are not difficult to see. The religion of the first type (Monarchianism) easily becomes a matter of obedience to a remote God (almost an absentee landlord of the Universe). The religion of the other type tends equally easily to become only a matter of a restricted, localized, and therefore often exaggerated, devotion.

And both of them tend to suggest that the focus of religion is *away* from the world of real life as it is lived from day to day. That which they both need is just that which full Trinitarian faith exists to convey: the sense of the presence of God, carrying all the content of the Biblical revelation, present and active as Spirit.

We can, I believe, go further. It is a commonplace to say that the heart of the Christian Gospel is the affirmation that God is love. That is his nature, his being. The very fact that it is a commonplace means that we seldom stop to reflect on what it implies. Love is by definition a relationship. It cannot be exercised in isolation. If this is what we are meaning when we affirm that that is the essence of God's being, it carries a profoundly important implication. By contrast with the classical view of Greek philosophical thought which envisaged God as isolated in the contemplation of his own perfection, the Christian faith maintains that from all eternity there exists within the being of God an internal relationship which alone makes love possible. It is of course this thought which appears in that mysterious passage in our Lord's prayer on the last night of his life in which he speaks of the love with which God has loved him 'before the foundation of the world' (John 17:24). It looks as though the doctrine of the Trinity was not after all a mere theological puzzle, let alone a mathematical absurdity, but rather the attempt to give some kind of rationale of that which had become, through the revelation in Jesus, the deepest certainty in the faith of his friends.

CHAPTER 7

The Witness of History

I CONFESS that as I contemplated the writing of this chapter, my heart sank. That immortal work *The Descent of the Dove** contains 233 pages. At the end there is a chronological table. The first entry is 'Ascent of our Lord and Descent of the Holy Ghost'; the last is 'European War: second period of hostilities'. It takes a Charles Williams to do that kind of thing. Monsignor Ronald Knox found that he needed rather more space. *Enthusiasm*,† which, from its own particular angle, might not unfairly be regarded as a study of the tensions created in the Church by what men have claimed as irruptions of the Spirit, contains 591 pages. In what possible form, without gross superficiality, or even grosser misrepresentation, can one hope to trace the working of the Spirit through all the centuries which separate 'that first fine careless rapture' of the New Testament from our own perplexed and disillusioned age?

And yet the attempt must be made. These centuries contain the record of men's perception of the working of God's Spirit, outside as well as inside the bounds of the Church – often enough of their imperception. They illustrate the achievements made possible by response to that stirring; and the mistakes and dead-ends to which a misreading of its true character or a wilful disobedience to its guidance have led. And it is only in so far as we can gain even a limited insight into that record that we find a vantage-point from which to ask the questions which must occupy us in the concluding chapters. Where are we to discern the stirring of the Spirit of God, again outside as well as inside the life of the

* Charles Williams (Faber, 1950). † O.U.P., 1950.

Church, in our own day? By what criterion can we distinguish what *is* the working of the Spirit from the commotions caused by an outburst of emotional fervour, an impatient determination to set the world to rights 'without tarrying for any', or a claim to final illumination which will dispel the mists of superstition and bigotry and lead men forward into a millennium of enlightenment? And how, in an age which some hail and others bewail as 'post-Christian', can the Church vindicate again the claim that the power which is 'making all things new' is indeed that which in the Orthodox Liturgy is worshipped as 'the Spirit Holy, Lordly, Quickening'?

Clearly anything in the way of a chronological presentation is out of the question. Restrictions of space – let alone my own incapacity for such an undertaking – rule that out. Perhaps the best that can be done is to take up certain clues which have already presented themselves in our study of the New Testament evidence, and see whether, as we follow them up, we can discover some kind of track which leads through the confused record of advance and relapse, of fidelity and apostasy, a track marked by the persistent impulsion of the Spirit, recalling men to truth, pointing them forward to the apprehension of new truth.

At the outset we had better forewarn ourselves by remembering the hint dropped in the preceding chapter. The formative period of Christian doctrinal thought, which covers the greater part of the first five centuries, paid in the main scant attention to the person and work of the Spirit. It was preoccupied with other equally vital aspects of Christian faith, notably the doctrines of Incarnation and Atonement. And it is not to be wondered at if this comparative neglect to give to the Spirit his proper place in the Christian apprehension of the being of God provided an unpromising start from which the Church has found it difficult to recover; or if that intellectual disinterest is reflected in much of the worship and life of the Church. The Spirit has indeed throughout been the inspiration and driving force of the Church's life. But it has been an inspiration working often enough against the dominant trends of belief and practice, an under-current of vitality which has only revealed itself when it has burst through to the surface in the form of protests, reforms, revivals, upheavals.

Our New Testament study disclosed certain key-words in which the earliest Christian community described the ways in which the working of the Spirit had made itself felt. Freedom, illumination, power, grace (the fruit of the Spirit), unity: and all of them hall-marked, as it were, by the fact that they were gifts of the Spirit of *Jesus*. They were to be true to type. They were to reflect those graces as they had been demonstrated in that life. Only so would they be distinguished from the spurious forms which in the life of any Church can only too easily usurp their place. And they were all bestowed within the compass of the last and greatest of them, unity, by which alone they could be used 'for the common good', instead of, as so often, being made instruments of sectional, partisan, or even individual self-assertion. It is not difficult to see the same continuing power at work in the never-ending struggle to keep alive in the Church these characteristic gifts against the constantly recurring temptation to betray or misuse them. We need not indeed expect to find that the evidence falls into a neat and tidy pattern; that particular movements of the Spirit in reform or renewal can be labelled as the reaction against this or that particular form of relapse. For in most of such situations the elements combine, often enough in surprising variations, to provoke a protest on more counts than one.

Freedom; liberation. There are many forms of bondage into which a Church can fall. The besetting danger of any institution is submergence under the increasing weight of legalism and formalism. The danger is inherent in the very situation. The life of a Church is bound to be institutional:

form and rules are of its essence. The idea that there can be
a 'religion of the Spirit' – if by that is meant a community
life which is wholly independent of order and regulation – is
one which has always been congenial to certain types of mind.
It is an illusion. But it is an illusion which draws its attractive-
ness and power from the realization that forms can only too
easily quench the Spirit.

Where that happens Christian liberty is threatened by a
variety of usurping powers. Men come to believe that moral
insight can be codified in canons and rules of conduct the
authority of which will render unnecessary a continuous
exercise of discernment and judgement both by the Christian
community and by the individual. Worship, which should
be worship in spirit and in truth, can come to be stereotyped
in ever more exactly regulated patterns, upon the due observance of which its efficacy is said to depend. The authoritative
body, with which rests the power to impose the rules and
prescribe the ceremonial, tends to become more and more an
authoritarian hierarchy, which resents and ultimately sup-
presses the demand of the individual soul for free access to
God.

Illumination: the power of the Spirit to lead men into
truth, to confirm in their mind and conscience that that
which they are asked to believe and have accepted, is indeed
the truth of God. It is easy to see how close is the connexion
between this prompting of the Spirit and the foregoing one.
For if men are tempted to fall back on something less than
the authority of moral and spiritual insight as the basis for
rules of conduct or forms of worship, they will easily be led
into a further and more disastrous error. They will try to
withhold or to ban access to the truth which, as they instinctively know, is the source of freedom. From this springs a
crop of evils. Church authorities seek to retain 'the key of
knowledge' in their own hands. It is easier to control and
direct a laity who are cut off from the understanding which

would enable them to criticize official pronouncements. More serious still, they will develop a purely defensive attitude against the infiltration of new studies and new insights which threaten the established positions. Hence the long and dismal history of the refusal to recognize the working of God's Spirit alike in the first stirrings and in the relentless advance of the scientific revolution, and in the attempts of more enlightened and adventurous minds to enlist the new methods of inquiry in the service of a richer understanding of Christian faith and history.

Power. Here pre-eminently we can discern what is implied in the insistence that the Spirit is the Spirit of Jesus. From the first, in his realization and acceptance of the terms in which Messiahship must be understood and lived out, he had rejected once and for all the solicitation to use any of the secular forms of power on which religion is tempted to rely. For the early centuries it had been comparatively easy, through sheer force of circumstances, for the Church to escape the first of these temptations. A tolerated or persecuted minority is at least free from this danger. It was only when the entire position was reversed by the recognition of Christianity as the religion of the Empire that the Church found itself exposed to its full force. From then onwards in every variety of form the danger has been present. There has been the lure of alliance with the dominant power, be it sovereign prince or political party. There has been the tendency to become so closely identified with a particular order of society or with the fortunes of a particular nation or race, that it has become difficult if not impossible for the Church to preserve the true independence of the Gospel, and to exercise a prophetic ministry. There has been the crude material temptation to amass wealth, and to reckon power in terms of prosperity. Most degrading of all has been the use of temporal power in the preservation of the Church's rights and in the propagation of the Gospel itself. There may indeed be truth in the

contention that to persecute and be persecuted, to be willing
to kill and to die, in defence of faith is better evidence of the
vitality of religion than the indifference which would never
think of going to such lengths. But it none the less remains
a fact that religious persecution and the wars of religion are
the most terrible denials of Christianity which history can
show.

Grace: the growth in Christian character. Here indeed we
might feel that the issue was clear. It is possible for men to
resist the demands of freedom under a mistaken sense of the
need to preserve order and authority. It is possible, indeed
natural, for them to shrink from the sometimes unwelcome
and disturbing impact of new knowledge, which may seem
to threaten the foundations of faith. It can even be that, faced
with opposition which if successful could destroy the very
existence of the Church, they may feel justified in having
recourse to means of defence the use of which would be
difficult to reconcile with the Gospel. But on this issue of
accepting or refusing the ideal of character set before men in
the Gospel, there can surely be no possibility of equivocation
or self-deception. Grievous falling short, even flat denial, of
the Christian standard there will be, since human nature
always stands in need of redemption. But when men set themselves with earnestness and devotion to strive after the attainment of holiness, when they deliberately invoke the Spirit as
their guide in seeking to attain to a higher level of goodness,
then surely we may hope to see the outcome which we should
expect.

And yet, *corruptio optimi pessima*. There is sad evidence in
the pages of Church history, from the Montanist movement
onwards through recurrent outbreaks of 'Perfectionism', that
the desire for a severer standard of morality, the aspiration
towards a higher level of holiness, can be distorted in ways
which lead to results almost exactly the opposite of those
which were intended. It can be seen not only in the more

extravagant forms of fanaticism, but in too many instances in which the conviction of a higher spirituality has blinded men to the claims of charity and toleration, and has produced a temper which condemns the world, and even repudiates the merits of fellow-Christians.

Honesty compels the acknowledgement of failures to respond, and even of resistances to the working of the Spirit such as these. But it would be a mere travesty of the truth to suggest that the evidence is all on the debit side. Periods of decline have constantly evoked movements of recovery. The evangelization of heathen Europe, the preservation of worship and learning in the monastic life, the protest of the Reformers against moral abuses and theological error, the slow patient struggle for freedom and enlightenment in Biblical interpretation, the 'saving of England for Christianity' by the Methodist revival, the radical reforms in worship of the Liturgical Movement within the Roman Catholic Church, above all the world-wide urge towards the recovery of unity, are clear evidence of the unceasing impulsion of the Spirit.

And if – almost at random – we take a few illustrations of this driving force at work, these may perhaps serve.

It may seem at once a little strange, and too easy, to select Francis of Assisi for the first. There is here no spectacular revolt against Church authority: indeed from the first, and, at whatever cost of inner misgiving, throughout, Francis behaved as a humble and loyal son of the Church. And on the other hand the story has been so overlaid with the sentimentalism which too often dogs the footsteps of saintliness that the cutting edge of its challenge can easily be lost.

The obvious appeal of the Franciscan movement is the acceptance of poverty. But that very fact is also something which sets it above the level of discipleship which the ordinary man, or indeed the Church as a whole, feels to be possible. It becomes the high and special calling of a select few. Whereas

surely the heart of the renunciation, the motive which gives
it its distinctively Christian quality, is that the acceptance of
poverty is the symbol of an entire refusal to rely on *power* of
any kind save that which is inherent in self-giving love. It is
the repudiation not only of the obvious and vulgar estimate
of the Church's strength by the yardstick of wealth and influence, but of the far more subtle danger of reliance upon,
and even identification with, a ruling power, a political party,
an economic order of society, even an ecclesiastical system.
And this is a challenge which must be faced by the Church as
a whole and by every individual member of it. It demands
the most ruthless examination of every programme and policy,
whether at the highest level of the Church's relation to the
State, or at the humbler level of local politics and administration, to make sure that in the supposed interests of the Church's
prestige and success we are not betraying and surrendering the
one power on which as Christians we have the right to rely.

But it goes deeper still. There is a definite point at which
the issue of *poverty* becomes relevant. The demand of social
justice for a more equitable sharing of the good things of life
is one which the Christian conscience must clearly accept.
But it is a demand which can be distorted, and in subtle ways.
It is not difficult to detect here and there in contemporary
political attitudes, notably in the sphere of education, the
demand that nobody shall enjoy anything that everybody
cannot share. The Christian attitude, as depicted in Francis,
is the precise reverse. I will not allow myself to enjoy that
which others lack. That indeed is a truth which Churches
need to take home to their conscience. Nobody who considers
the proportionate outlay on the maintenance and adornment
of our churches at home, and on the maintenance and expansion of the Church's work overseas, can escape the condemna-
tion implied in the Franciscan sense of proportion. Few of us
in our individual assessment of our own needs as against those
of others are in much better case.

The world of seventeenth-century Protestantism was a strange tangle – one might almost write jungle – of fanatical sects, Anabaptists and Ranters, Mennonites and The Family of Love, Brownists and Collegiants. 'Into this world of discredited sects,' writes Monsignor Knox,

with the air of a liberator, strides in the giant figure of George Fox, the man in leather breeches. These muddy pools of forlorn controversy shall be the culture from which new life is to be infused into the religion of England. ... His stature is somehow heroic. Allow if you will for a certain amount of exaggeration when he tells you, in the Journal, how instantaneous were the effects of his preaching, how easily he put his adversaries to silence; discount the egotism, if you can call it egotism, of a man wholly absorbed in his mission. Remember only that this is a man, full of scruples and questionings in his youth who without (it seems) any agonies of conversion has emerged into a state of complete spiritual equilibrium, is sure of himself in all companies and on all occasions. Watch him walking barefoot through the streets of a Cathedral town, ingeminating 'Woe to the bloody city of Lichfield', interrupting the sermons of the ministers in their steeple-houses, and preaching at them from the floor of the church, allowing street-boys to pelt him and roll him in the mud, lecturing the magistrates when he appears before them, refusing to eat meat with the Lord Protector after his interview. ... And his companions how they multiply. ... They go everywhere; they try to convert a Pope, they try to convert a Sultan. In a fury of disagreement with all they see around them they carry the stout protest of their covered heads before magistrates and councils, before Kings and princes of the earth.

'In a fury of disagreement with all they see around them.' It is impossible to fit the crusade of the original Friends into the strait-jacket of a protest against any one of the abuses in the life of the Church: indeed, they are almost as violent in their denunciation of civil authorities as of 'priests and professors'. But at the heart of George Fox's obstinate, often exasperating, 'non-conformity' there lies one passionate conviction. The religion of his day is not meeting men's need, it is not 'speaking to their condition'. In the light of the direct experience which has been given to him he can insist that 'God himself was come to teach his people by his Spirit and to bring them off all their old ways, religions, Churches and worship. For all their religions and worship and ways was but talking of other men's words, but they was out of the life and spirit that they was in that gave them forth.'

He can say to Margaret Fell, 'What had any to do with the Scriptures, but as they came to the Spirit who gave them forth? You will say, Christ saith this, and the Apostles this; but what canst thou say?'

The doctrine of the Inner Light, clear and convincing enough in the experience of Fox and his earlier followers, has proved to be less easy to maintain as the guiding principle of faith and action for a whole community. The fact that the Society has, almost of deliberate purpose, failed to relate it to the main stream of Christian theology has been one of the causes which has kept the Friends isolated from the main body of Christendom, in a way which has lessened the influence which their superb witness to social righteousness has deserved. But their distinctive ethos, as in the case of the Franciscans, stands as an abiding testimony of the power of the Spirit to bring new life into the Church, and as a continuing reminder of spiritual truth which the Church forgets at its peril.

There could at first glance scarcely be a greater contrast, in the outward circumstances of early upbringing and education, than that between George Fox and John Wesley. On the one hand the weaver's cottage at Drayton in the Clay, the apprenticeship to the shoe-maker 'who dealt in wool, used grazing and sold cattle', the solitary childhood and youth, culminating in the sudden decision when 'at the command of God, on the ninth day of the seventh month 1643, I left my relations, and brake off all familiarity or fellowship with old or young'. And on the other the cultured background of the rectory at Epworth, with its busy family life, the steady educational progress from Charterhouse to Christ Church, the coaching in advance in Hebrew by elder brother Samuel at Westminster, the Fellowship at Lincoln with the Lectureship in Greek, and the Moderatorship of the Classes in Disputation.

But the contrast is in many ways more apparent than real. In both men from early years there is the same unmistakable evidence of spiritual dissatisfaction with the religious and moral climate in which they find themselves living. In as real a sense, though the manner of doing it was different, Wesley broke off relationship with his world. 'When it pleased God to give me a settled resolution to be not a nominal but a real Christian, my acquaintance were as ignorant of God as myself. But there was this difference: I knew my own ignorance; they did not know theirs. ... Entering now as it were into a new world' (on the election to Lincoln) 'I resolved to have no acquaintance by chance but by choice, and to choose only such as I had reason to believe would help me on my way to heaven.' Incipient signs of the perfectionist, the separatist, even the prig? Maybe; but it is a plain fact of history that it is often men who feel such a call and who are prepared to accept the consequences of such a course of action, who are used by the Spirit to achieve a break-out or a break-through. 'I knew many reflections would follow; but that did not move me, as I knew full well that it was my calling to go *through evil report and good report*.' And the incredible record of the succeeding sixty years – courage, endurance, devotion, unceasing activity – is evidence enough that the call was genuine and that it was accepted without counting the cost.

It cannot be claimed that in the immense volume of preaching material which Wesley left behind him the work of the Spirit holds a central place. For one whose primary passion was evangelism it was natural that the fact of Christ and his redemptive power should be the dominant theme. But none the less there are clear indications that in some of the most characteristic notes of his message it was to the Spirit that he looked as the distinctive power.

There is a series of five sermons * on 'The First-Fruits of the Spirit' and 'The Witness of the Spirit' which illustrate convincingly that combination of close reasoning and penetrating appeal which characterizes so much of his preaching. He is under no illusions as to the dangers which attend a facile assumption of the possession of the Spirit. 'How many men have mistaken the voice of their own imagination for this witness of the Spirit of God, and thence idly presumed that they were children of God, while they were doing the works of the devil! These are truly and properly "enthusiasts", and indeed in the worst sense of the word. But with what difficulty are they convinced thereof.... Who then can be surprised if many reasonable men seeing the dreadful effects of this delusion, and labouring to keep at the utmost distance from it, should sometimes lean to another extreme?' (Had he Bishop Butler in mind when he wrote these words?) But having recognized the danger, he will not allow it to deter him from insisting on the necessity for the recognition of the testimony of God's Spirit in a man's soul as the essential condition of a truly converted Christian life. 'Without busying ourselves in curious needless enquiries touching those *extraordinary* gifts of the Spirit, let us take a nearer view of those his ordinary fruits ... of that great work of God among the children of men which we are used to express by one word, *Christianity*, not as it implies a set of opinions, a system of doctrines, but as it refers to men's hearts and lives.' 'It' (the purpose of Pentecost) 'was to give men the mind which was in Christ, those holy fruits of the Spirit, which whoever hath not is none of his ... to enable them to walk as Christ walked in the work of faith, in the patience of hope, the labour of love.'

* *Sermons*, ed. John Beecham, vol. 1. Sermons viii–xii.

And there is the tremendous sermon * preached from the pulpit of the University Church at Oxford in which he calls both City and University to examine their consciences. 'Let me ask you then, in tender love and in the spirit of meekness, Is this City a Christian City? Is Christianity, scriptural Christianity, found here? Are we, considered as a community of men, so "filled with the Holy Ghost" as to enjoy in our hearts and show forth in our lives the genuine fruits of that Spirit? Are all the Magistrates, all Heads and Governors of Colleges and Halls, and their respective Societies, "of one heart and one soul"? Is "the love of God shed abroad in our hearts"? Are our tempers the same that were in him? And are our lives agreeable thereto?'

But it is less in his preaching or his writings that the witness of the Spirit is to be seen than in the sheer quality of the man, and in the impact of his work upon the life of England.

The recorded figures of his travelling and preaching are almost legendary. Here is just one example – a record of places visited in 136 consecutive days in one year out of fifty. 'Bristol, Monday March 19th 1774 I set out for the North. Saturday, August 4th, we crossed the New Passage and rode on to Bristol.' And there follows a list of 128 towns and villages from Stroud to Inverness and back covered in 1,800 miles of riding, in each of which he preached, often more than once a day.

It is not difficult, in the light of insights which have become more familiar to us from the experience of the nineteenth and twentieth centuries, to point out limitations in Wesley's Gospel. He was the child of his own century, the philosophy of which minimized the influence of environment and made him indifferent to the conditions under which men had to live. The Hammonds in *The Town Labourer* can remark, somewhat superciliously, that 'the Methodist Movement was a call not for citizens but for saints'. The fact remains that

* *Sermons*, vol. 3. Sermon iv.

into the lives of thousands, in whom neither the established Church nor state institutions showed any human interest, his preaching and personal care brought a message of hope, the possibility and the reality of a new life of decency and self-respect.

As one reads the story one's mind instinctively reverts to the revealing quotation from *La Princesse lointaine* with which Monsignor Knox ends his study of the perils of 'enthusiasm':

Frère Trophime: L'inertie est le seul vice, Maître Érasme;
   Et la seule vertu est …
Érasme: Quoi?
Frère Trophime: L'enthousiasme!

The three illustrations which we have taken have been instances of the work of individual men. They differ widely in their historical setting and in the character of their respective contributions. They all exemplify the fact that it is from such individual beginnings, from the power of the Spirit to fasten on an individual soul, that movements are born which expand into world-wide forces and influence the whole pattern of religious life for succeeding generations.

For our last illustration we may take a different type. The great missionary movement of the last hundred and fifty years can indeed point to a handful of outstanding personalities as its pioneers. But its essential character is that it has caught up into its advance a host of men and women, drawn from every walk of life, representing every section of the Christian Church. Its true significance is to be seen in the diversity of its agencies within the single unifying passion for the spread of the Gospel.

Within this short span of time it has altered out of all recognition the pattern of Christian expansion throughout the world. In 1800 with a few isolated exceptions the greater part of Asia and Africa was untouched by Christian influence. The Christian Church was confined within the frontiers of the Western world. Today there is scarcely an area in those two continents and beyond in which there is not to be found a Christian Church – would God it were *one* Christian Church! – which has become or is becoming indigenous. The earlier distinction between sending and receiving Churches has become out of date. Representatives of the Christian community in India and Pakistan, in Malaya and Japan, in the Middle East and Africa meet as equal partners with the representatives of the Church in the West, and share with them the responsibilities of a common enterprise.

From this missionary expansion have sprung insights and influences which have radically affected our whole understanding of the nature of the Gospel and of the Church.

Slowly, and as yet only very imperfectly, there has come home to the Christian conscience the inescapable truth that, in the light of the New Testament, the life of the Church is Mission. A Church which is engrossed in the maintenance of its own internal life, which is not looking outwards and seeking to make the truth as it is in Jesus available for all men, may indeed be a flourishing institution. But it is not the Church of God. The evangelistic impulse which alone sustains and invigorates the Christian community in India or Africa is beginning to seep back into the life of the Church in this country. It may indeed well be that we in the West will have to relearn some of the elementary lessons of Christian discipleship from those to whom we taught them.

And almost as a by-product, though a by-product of even greater significance, there has come the realization that this, the essential task of the Church, cannot be accomplished by a Church which is divided. It is not without reason that so many accounts of the Oecumenical Movement start with the Missionary Conference at Edinburgh in 1910. For beyond any question the real urgency of the drive towards the recovery of unity has come from the younger Churches, who have discovered that their very life depends upon the elimination of the sinful waste of division, and are telling us in no uncertain terms that they desire to set their house in order in this matter, and at a more rapid pace than seems to be tolerated in our leisurely negotiations at home.

It would be misguided to claim too much for what has been achieved in this last century and a half. No one with any insight into the effects on the Church, whether at home or overseas, of these last forty-five years with their exposure of the 'Christian West', and the disruptive forces which Communism and Nationalism have unleashed on the world, will be in any doubt as to their seriousness. It is easy to draw parallels from history and to ask whether, as before, the Christian Church in this or that area of the world may not be overrun and wiped out. It is possible to ask whether the original evangelistic impulse has not already spent its force. The answer is, I believe, to be found in the recognition of the fact that the Spirit of God is at work, reckoning with these revolutionary forces and teaching the Christian mind to learn from set-backs and dangers lessons which it had not grasped in the earlier periods of enthusiasm and success. We are learning that mere geographical expansion is not necessarily the secret of true advance or consolidation. We are learning that the very character of the earlier evangelism, with its tendency to an exclusive emphasis on individual conversion, and its comparative disregard of social, cultural, and economic elements may have contained seeds of weakness. We are learning that there are other forms of Christian infiltration and permeation which need to be explored and developed if a Christian community, a Christian society, is to be established on alien ground.

'A tactical regrouping of our forces' was a phrase in war communiqués often suspected as a euphemism for a nasty set-back, if not a defeat. It may well be that the Christian Church has had, and will have, to face experiences of this kind. But no one who has studied the history of this last century and a half, no one who has seen at first-hand, even if only very briefly, the working of the Spirit in the remaking of human life and the fashioning of Christian fellowship within the sphere of Christian mission, is in any doubt that a flame has been kindled which will not be put out.

CHAPTER 8

'*Your God is Too Small*'

How constantly the phrase which Canon J. B. Phillips chose as the title of that admirable little book* comes home to roost! Over and over again in different contexts one finds oneself being pulled up short by the realization that it is just precisely the restrictedness, the inadequacy, of our conception of God which is the cause of the Church's failure to meet some new demand, to get to grips with some fresh problem arising from the ever-changing climate of thought.

Most notably is this true in the particular context with which this book is concerned. The preceding chapter sought to present just a few snapshots of the impact of the Spirit throughout fourteen centuries of Church history. But it was *Church* history. The illustrations were drawn from the lives of men who had exercised an outstanding influence in the religious life of their own age, and had by so doing left a permanent mark. Even the world-wide missionary movement could be seen to be subject in some respects to the same limitation, and to be for that very reason handicapped in its attempt to permeate and influence the spheres of cultural and political life. It might well have seemed that the Spirit of God was to be discerned as active only within the bounds of the ecclesiastical world, that his influence was only to be seen in the shaping of conciliar decisions, in the awakening of a theological or doctrinal revival, in the expansion of the geographical area of Christendom.

Here indeed we reach a point of very real difficulty. It would, I think, be hard to resist the conclusion that so far as the New Testament and the bulk of patristic thought are

* Epworth Press, 1952.

concerned, the Spirit *is* presented as primarily at work in the conversion and enlightenment of the individual soul and in the building up of the corporate life of those who have been received into the redeemed community. A moment's recollection will make it clear that this is largely understandable when we consider the actual circumstances of the Christian society which these writings reflect. But if there is truth in the indications (suggested in the preceding chapter) of the dangers to which, throughout its history, the Church has been exposed through its refusal to acknowledge and respond to the promptings of the Spirit, the implication is obvious. The Church can never be truly 'led by the Spirit' unless it is continually alive to the fact that the world is God's world, that he is always and everywhere present in creation and the shaping of history, and that the signs of that presence are to be discerned, directly or indirectly, in movements which at first sight may often appear to be unrelated to, even in direct opposition to, the religious set-up of the time.

This chapter is frankly only a footnote. Like the preceding one it aims at no more than selecting one or two illustrations, in this case of the way in which the Christian mind, if it is to be true to the Old Testament prophetic tradition, and to its Master's injunction to 'discern the signs of the times', must be constantly sensitive to the 'secular' forces which are shaping the character of civilization and man's whole understanding of his nature as man.

That the Scientific Revolution is one such force is beyond question. The verdicts of Professor Butterfield and Sir Lawrence Bragg quoted in the opening chapter could be multiplied a hundredfold. A new factor in human history has emerged of incalculable range and potentiality. No aspect of life or thought, from our cosmogony to our genetics, can remain unaffected by its discoveries. It has begun, and will continue, to affect man's basic estimate of his standing in the universe.

And the crucial question which such a revolution poses for

the Christian mind is precisely: What *spiritual* evaluation of it do we give? Is it to be interpreted as the latest, some would say the ultimate, expression of Titanism, of man's revolt against all divine authority, the rebellion which must inevitably bring its own nemesis? Or do we discern in it an immensely significant prompting of that same Spirit which, as Christians believe, has throughout the ages been at work in bringing to birth at every stage a fuller development of powers inherent in the nature of man as child of God?

Of course that antithesis states the case in crudely black and white terms. But I have no doubt in my own mind which of the two views is *nearer* to a Christian verdict. And I am convinced that it is only as the Church adopts a positive attitude, ceases to deplore and sets itself to understand, that it will be in a position to make any effective *Christian* contribution to the right direction of these immense powers.

The nature of that contribution will obviously be the making of a Christian critique, not so much of the actual findings of scientific discovery, as of the assumptions on which its method is based, and of the adequacy both of assumptions and method for a full interpretation of man's nature and destiny. Dr Oldham* illustrates the point by a reference to Professor Weizsäcker's *The History of Nature*. The vast accumulation of scientific knowledge, he reminds us, has its source in the mind of man. Man is part of nature, but without man there would be no knowledge of nature. We cannot separate our knowledge of nature from our knowledge of man. But between the two forms of knowledge there is a profound difference. Man is undoubtedly in part an object in nature, and can be studied like other objects. But he is not only that. He is also a subject who knows and has to make decisions. 'He finds himself faced with demands made on him, demands that he must follow or reject. Misery, anguish and hope, love and hate, custom and conscience, fellow-man

---

* *Life is Commitment* (S.C.M., 1953), p. 20.

and God, make demands on him. Much of man's knowledge of himself can be expressed properly not as a statement but as an imperative.' Our knowledge of nature, and our knowledge of man, he adds, are like two half-circles which need 'to be joined together in such a way that they combine to form a full circle, and this circle ought then to be followed round fully many times.'

It is of course a familiar point. But the essential condition of its fulfilment is the recognition that the two forms of knowledge, though diverse in kind, spring from a common source. They are knowledge of the one universe. And that one universe is God's.

To take another illustration: readers of Nicolas Berdyaev's autobiography will remember the chapter in which he describes his experiences during the early days of the Communist revolution, and seeks to disentangle the strands of his own spiritual reaction to it. Here is a man who combines in himself the highest levels of European culture, a passionate sense of social justice, and a profound, if highly individualistic and often unorthodox, Christian conviction. For him there was no superficial black and white judgement on the significance of the revolution. He was under no illusions as to the true character and possible implications of such an upheaval. 'A revolution is, in fact, a serious disease and source of agony to those who undergo it: it is a symptom of creative disablement, of a neglected responsibility, or of the responsibility incurred by doing nothing.'* On the other hand he was equally unable to align himself with the tendency to regard the revolution as 'something brought about by the powers of evil, and perpetrated by a band of criminal maniacs.' 'I did not conceal my attitude to communism. Indeed I waged an open war against its spirit, or rather against its hostility to the spirit. Least of all did I desire restoration. I was entirely convinced that the old world had come to an end, and that a

* *Dream and Reality* (Bles, 1950). See especially chapter 9.

return to it was alike impossible and undesirable.... I was convinced that the guilt and responsibility for the horrors of the revolution lay above all on the men of the old regime.... Later I came to realize that the leaders of the Russian renascence, of whom I was one, also had their share in the guilt of the hostile attitude of the Russian revolution towards spiritual values: we were guilty of softness, of social irresponsibility, self-sufficiency, and pseudo-aristocratism. The supreme responsibility, however, lies with historical Christianity and with Christians, who have failed to fulfil their duty. Communism was for me from the start a challenge and a reminder of an unfulfilled Christian duty. Christians ought to have embodied the truth of communism: had they done so, its falsehood would never have won the day.'

No one who has lived through the forty years since the Russian Revolution will be under any illusions as to the horrors which it has involved for millions of its victims, or as to the threat which communism in its present form presents to mankind as a whole. And it will seem to many an outrageous, almost a blasphemous, paradox to suggest that such a movement could have been, even in its initial impulse, an expression of the working of God's Spirit. None the less I find myself impelled by Berdyaev's argument to face certain inescapable questions.

When we examine honestly the record of the Church as, among other things, the instrument of God's will for the 'blessedness', the wholeness of life of all humanity; when we consider the centuries in which in the main the Church has been blind and deaf to that aspect of its duty, is it possible *not* to see in the uprisings of men against tyranny, callous neglect of human rights, tolerance of intolerable wrong, an outbreaking of the Spirit of God who works through judgement as well as through mercy?

And if there be even a measure of truth in that assessment, what does it involve for the spiritual strategy of the Church as it finds itself confronted by the consequences of the communist impact right across the world? There is no quick and easy answer. Indeed it is likely enough that there will have to be a number of answers, which will vary with the different circumstances of the encounter in East Germany, or China, or Africa. But always there will be, as I would judge, the tension which arises in the Christian conscience from the recognition of two facts, neither of which can be denied. There is the fact of human sin, as that exhibits itself in the particular forms which are apparent in communist tyranny. But there is also the fact that the tyranny which we condemn and seek to break is itself in its essence a violent protest against other forms of sin present in other forms of society and in the life of the Church as involved in those forms of society.

May it not be that it is something of this kind which is implied in that mysterious saying of the Lord that 'When the Spirit has come he will convict the world in respect of sin and of righteousness and of judgement'? He speaks of the Spirit convicting the *world*. Do we go beyond his meaning if we extend that conviction to include the Church?

'Your God is too small.' Is there not here an exposure of that individualism which so often restricts the convicting work of the Spirit to the sphere of the individual conscience? People of undoubted piety and uprightness of character can sometimes be strangely blind to the fact that, whatever the level of their private life, they are involved in the sin of their world, and of their church. Unquestionably that was true of some of the outstanding religious figures of the nineteenth century who cultivated a high degree of piety while their fellow-Christians rotted in slums. But we need not delude ourselves with the belief that we have outgrown their shortsightedness. The acid test of the genuineness of Christian profession today is to be found for instance in our concern for the impact of our civilization upon the peoples of Africa. It is all too easy to profess, and indeed to practise, a devout churchmanship, and to turn a blind eye to Hola and Sharpeville.

CHAPTER 9

The Vindication of Christian Faith

I INDICATED in the opening chapter some of the critical solvents to which the Christian faith, which means the whole Christian view of man's life as created, directed, and redeemed by God, is exposed today; solvents, in the judgement of many, more radical than any which have threatened it in the past.

Some of the criticism takes the form of definite attack. Marxism, by its very presuppositions, is committed to the extirpation of what it regards as superstition, calculated, if not deliberately designed and exploited, to maintain the dominance of a privileged class by the suppression of truth, freedom, and justice. Much more of the criticism takes the form of a more or less contemptuous dismissal of religion as a relic of a primitive stage of man's development in which his ignorance of the real nature of his world made him the prey of those fears and delusions from which, on this view, belief in supernatural power springs. He has now 'come of age'. He has emerged into a stage of scientific and economic enlightenment in which he can see that his former attitude of dependence on a power other and greater than his own was only a slavish relic, to be dispensed with if he is to advance into the full freedom which is his natural destiny.

Others, as we saw, while finding themselves equally unable to give honest and meaningful assent to Christian belief, as they have understood it, regard the disappearance of faith with concern and even dismay. They are conscious not only of the loss of something which has given to them as individuals encouragement and consolation. That they might face, if they were convinced that it had only been meant to be a support on which they might lean while they learned to face the demands of 'real life'. But it goes much deeper than that. They look for an alternative which will supply that which for believers religion does supply. Some of them seek it in the austere discipline of scientific research, or the costly struggle for social justice. But they do not always find in either of them the sense of being caught up into an eternal purpose, which offers them the challenge of what Reinhold Niebuhr calls 'an impossible ethical ideal', and at the same time gives significance and worth to what they recognize as their own short-lived, limited, and often partially frustrated efforts. And they sense, in this personal experience of their own, the dis-appearance of a 'dimension of depth', which means an impoverishment of all human life.

If these are some of the challenges and needs which confront the Church from outside, what of the internal situation? How do 'the faithful' – and in their loyalty and service many of them are indeed faithful – how do they stand in the matter of *faith* itself? I fancy that the position is more precarious than is often realized; and the reason for it is to be found in two grave shortcomings of us clergy. We are often criticized for our failure to understand the layman's point of view. Worse, we are often charged with the far greater fault of trying to turn him into a slightly inferior imitation of ourselves. It is painfully true that far too little thought has been given to the needs, and the potentialities, of those who constitute the vast majority of Christians, who have to express their faith in terms of 'secular' life. And it is equally true that the clergy can go sadly astray through expecting of lay people a 'theo-logical' apprehension of the faith, in a technical form which is only appropriate to those who have received the necessary training.

These two failures have, I believe, produced a situation which is almost as serious a danger to the vitality of Church life as any of the external menaces. Because we have not

realized or understood the 'lay' environment in which ordinary people have to work out the meaning and application
of their faith, we have failed to present Christian doctrine
in a form in which it can relate itself to, 'incarnate' itself
in, actual day-to-day situations. 'Creation', 'Atonement',
'Eternal Life' remain, for too many, propositions, to be
accepted as such. They do not become what they are, insights
into the nature of God's working in the world and in human
life. Belief in God as Creator never translates itself into a
realization of man's responsibility towards the material
resources of the natural world. Atonement never actualizes
itself as the experience of God's power to deal with the tragic
situations of an industrial conflict or racial strife or a broken
home. Eternal Life remains a distant and shadowy expecta-
tion, instead of the yardstick by which we measure all the
programmes and policies and values of life here and now.

And this absence, not of technical knowledge, but of understanding, insight, and appropriation, involves a grave weakening of the witness which lay people can and should make
to the reality of their faith. They are running on two cylinders
instead of four. Piety and 'Church work' are operating,
intelligent conviction and responsible action much less so.
And the result is too often a Church quiescent rather than
militant, to all appearances largely insensitive to the stirring
of new thought and experiment, concerned more with the
maintenance of its own established life, than with meeting
the urgent, often desperate, needs of the world outside. Jesus
said of his Church: 'The gates of hell shall not prevail against
it.' But this sounds like a storming party attacking a strongly
held position rather than a garrison on the defensive within
its own perimeter.

It is the contention of these concluding chapters that the
only way in which the Church can recover the initiative
which rightly belongs to it as the instrument of God's truth
and saving power is by the recovery, maybe even the dis-

covery, of the reality of the Spirit: God in action, God contemporary and instant. Such an insight alone, as I believe, can give us the open-mindedness to acknowledge God at work in the revolutionary changes in human knowledge and understanding, and the ferment of social ideas to which they give rise, *and* the discernment to distinguish and identify what is the evidence of his working in these spheres and what is not. The same insight alone can give us the faith and readiness for risk, which are the essential conditions of an effective response.

I want in this chapter to think about what should be the response of a Church which is 'living in the Spirit' to the intellectual situation created by the climate of our time. Our consideration must reckon with two forms of challenge. There is that which arises directly from the criticisms of those who have abandoned, or have never accepted, the Christian position. And there is also the less easily defined problem of the state of mind of 'believers' whose faith has been disturbed – dare one add, ought to have been disturbed? – by the subtle influences of an environment of doubt and uncertainty.

To begin with the first of the two. It is, needless to say, preposterous to suppose that in half a chapter one can deal in any detail with the particular problems which are raised by contemporary scientific and philosophical thought. Each of these groups of problems would require full-scale treatment in a book to itself. All that one can hope to do is to suggest some ways in which a Church which is sensitively alive to the situation can shape an appropriate response to the demand which it makes.

The clue here is given in one of the most familiar sayings reported in the Fourth Gospel: 'When he, the Spirit of Truth, is come, he will guide you into truth in its entirety.' So William Temple translates John 16:13. And he adds this comment: 'There is of course no reference intended to the discovery of scientific or general historical truth: though in

E

as much as all truth of any kind must ultimately be one, that thought is not at all alien from what is intended.'* We may accept the reservation in the first half of the sentence: but it is essential to give full value to the admission contained in the second. For here indeed we reach a crucial point in our whole study of the working of God's Spirit outside, as well as inside, the bounds of what is commonly regarded as 'Church life'. Here we reach the need for that sensitive perception which can detect the stirring of the Spirit in other than religious or theological realms, and can welcome, *with discrimination*, the contribution of the scientist, the philosopher, the historian, and the artist.

The first essential for a Christian response to the intellectual environment will be one of active and sympathetic interest, not of fear, or hostility, or indifference. Those who are working in these other fields will be seen as partners, potential allies, not as suspected enemies, even when their work appears to lead to conclusions difficult indeed to reconcile with the traditional Christian interpretation of life.

In one of Mr Langmead Casserley's books the remark is made: 'A theologian is a man possessed of an insatiable curiosity which compels him to interest himself in everything in which he finds other men interested.' The natural instinct of the Christian, whose professional business it is to elucidate and expound the Christian faith, should be able to get alongside men engaged in other professional studies in order to discover what they have found in their exploration. Equally of course he will be anxious, if he can persuade them to regard it as worth their while to listen, to share with them the results of his own research.

Both sides will likely enough find that, in the early stages of such intercommunication, the going is slow and even painful. The remark of my young physicist, who when em-

* Temple, *Readings in St John's Gospel* (Macmillan, 1949), vol. 2, p. 290.

barking on the study of theology found it no easy matter to discover something which he could recognize as a 'fact', is typical of the difficulties which have to be surmounted in finding a common universe of discourse, literally in understanding one another's language. But all the time, if the inquiry is being pursued in the spirit of true research, with the humility which recognizes that truth is never to be found wholly on one side of the argument, there will be the driving force of the desire to get inside the other mind, to discover what makes it tick, to reach that point at which both participants can find some common point of firm standing ground of which they can say, 'Yes, I recognize that; we can start from there.'

In this process both sides will have to be prepared to expose themselves to a severe process of criticism and self-examination. Readers of Mr Hepburn's *Christianity and Paradox* will be under no illusions as to the tests which an analytical philosopher will insist on applying to theological statements. And equally readers of Mr George Woods's *Theological Explanation* will realize, with wonder and admiration, the patient step-by-step verification and 'explanation' by which the Christian advocate must be prepared to advance if he is to pass those tests. But my main reason for citing these two instances is that from their very different starting points they both exhibit precisely that temper of honest and realistic determination to get at truth, which I believe that both would be prepared to recognize as 'being led by the Spirit'.

In the early stages the Christian apologist may well seem to be mainly on the defensive. And it will do us no harm to have to look to our defences, and see that they are in as good order as we can make them. But of course we shall not remain on the defensive. There are plenty of questions, not less searching than some of those put to us, which we shall want to put to the other side. The going may not perhaps be quite so hard in the case of the natural scientists, or even the linguistic philosophers, who have in some respects appreciably modified their original criticisms. Our most pointed questions may well be reserved for the 'social' scientists who maintain that the methods of natural science can be applied *tout court* to human nature and its problems. Of them we shall certainly want to ask whether they seriously maintain the fantastic view that 'scientific method is the only generally accepted method of advancing our knowledge of anything'.* And we shall press home the question whether their basic assumption that the methods of investigation appropriate to the study of 'things' can be applied to the study of 'persons' is one which they are prepared to maintain consistently, in their dealings for instance with their own families. At the same time we shall of course recognize and give full value to the real contribution which their studies make to a more exact understanding and a more efficient handling of many of the environmental influences which a good deal of religious thinking has tended to ignore. For here again we shall thankfully acknowledge the unmistakable evidence of the Spirit leading men into essential truth.

This is clearly a 'top-level' undertaking. It can only be discharged by men whose scholarship commands the respect of their opposite numbers. But it calls for other gifts besides that of pure scholarship. There is in this task of intellectual reconciliation a truly pastoral aspect. In an unforgettable passage in the introduction to *Freedom and the Spirit* Berdyaev reveals something of the cost of returning to the Christian faith after a sojourn in the intellectual wilderness.

When a man returns to God after a period of apostasy he knows a freedom in his relations with him untasted by one who has passed his life in the peace and security of his traditional faith, and who has remained within the borders of his spiritual inheritance.

How, one may ask, are these travellers returning to the Father's

* Barbara Wootton, *Testament for Social Science* (Allen & Unwin, 1950), p. 54.

house received? Too often not in the way in which the Prodigal Son was welcomed. The voice of the Elder Son who boasts of having remained with the Father and of serving him is far too much in evidence. And yet among these pilgrims of the spirit there are not only the depraved: there are also those who are hungering and thirsting after truth. These will be accounted more righteous in the sight of God than numberless 'bourgeois Christians' who pride themselves on their Pharisaical religion and who imagine that they are 'men of property' in the religious sphere.*

It may indeed sound presumptuous to suggest that those with whom the Christian apologist is dealing should be regarded, or would regard themselves, as Prodigal Sons! But on the Christian side at least the point holds. There is need for a profound humility in our approach, a humility which springs from two sources. We shall recognize the extent to which their alienation from the Christian faith has been due to the inadequacies of our own presentation of it; and we shall equally recognize that their insights, as well as their doubts, may well point the way to a real clarification and enrichment.

It might sound as though the Church's work in this sphere was such as could only be carried on at a somewhat rarefied level by men and women possessing a high degree of specialized qualification. Such is not the case. This building up of a 'fellowship of Holy Spirit' which cuts right across the dividing line between 'believers' and 'unbelievers' is something which needs to be fostered at all levels. On a number of occasions in recent years I have asked representative groups of ordinary Church people to tell me how they defend and commend their faith in discussion with 'unbelievers'. It has been, to say the least of it, disconcerting to receive the reply that they don't think that they ever meet such people. It is difficult to avoid the conclusion that, so far as their religion is concerned, they are living in some kind of hermetically

* N. Berdyaev, *Freedom and the Spirit* (Bles, 1935), pp. viii, ix.

sealed chamber. And indeed one suspects that the insulation may well be of their own choosing, precisely because they feel that they would be quite unable to meet the demands of argument and controversy if they were to expose themselves to it.

This is a lamentable state of affairs which cannot be allowed to continue. It calls for definite and sustained action in two directions. There must be a deliberate and concerted effort on the part of the clergy to break down this spirit of defensiveness. Church people must be told that it is their business as Christians to get inside the minds of those among whom they live and work who are not Christians, in order that they may discover why they are not. Often enough this may best be done *not* by a direct approach on the religious front. The point of entry is far more likely to be some common problem of family life, business ethics, a concern for public affairs, which, seen in depth, raises questions of moral standards and convictions which up to a point are shared by both sides. Likely enough, once the talking point has been established, it will lead on to the discussion of matters of belief, or criticisms of the Church; and on these the doubter and the critic are very likely to give more serious consideration to the expressed convictions of fellow-laymen, who are not suspected of having a professional ecclesiastical axe to grind.

But – and it is a very large-sized but – any such development of lay strategy is impossible unless the second line of action is being taken simultaneously. The plain fact is that many of the laity are only too well justified in their fear that they are incompetent to undertake their proper task. And unless they are trained and equipped to do it far more adequately than at present, they had perhaps better not attempt it.

Here we reach the point at which we turn over to the second of the two problems with which I suggested that our consideration must deal: the state of mind of those who can, on the face of things at least, be reckoned as professing Christians.

It has been in the past the proud claim of the Church of England, and doubtless also of other Communions, to possess an instructed laity. It is doubtful how far that claim could today be justified. If, as the argument of this chapter would maintain, the Christian Church is engaged in an all-out battle, *at all levels*, for the vindication of its faith as a reasonable working interpretation of human life, which offers men, at the least, light in surrounding darkness and grace to supplement their own unreliable moral effort, then clearly we need the services of every available recruit. And those recruits will require equipment, and training in the use of it.

Here is a second undertaking no less urgent, and in some ways even more difficult, than the first. For as anyone with even a second-hand acquaintance with the theological situation today is well aware, theology itself is faced with a crop of unresolved problems of a highly technical character; and until some of these have been clarified, if not settled, it is extremely difficult to find ways and means of passing on to the rank and file of Church members a statement of the faith on which they can rely as at least reasonably guaranteed by authoritative scholarship.

To take one or two illustrations. We have on our hands the debate over Fundamentalism. And without entering into the niceties of defining just precisely what various brands of fundamentalists hold as the essential tenets of their creed, we can see only too plainly the serious effects of our uncertainty in the interpretation of the Bible upon the faith of rank and file believers. The fact that the Bible is now handled by the methods of historical and literary criticism is recognized. But very little of the exact details of that method, and still less of the sensitive temper required to give it balance, is understood. And the result is that large numbers of churchmen are left with a vague uneasy feeling that the authority and truth of the Bible have been undermined. If the story of the creation is a 'myth' (and they are not familiar with the proper meaning of that word), if Jonah and the whale is a parable, if the conclusions of some of the Parables are the not always very intelligent 'moral' drawn by a Christian preacher from the original story, and some of the elaborations of the Crucifixion story in Matthew are the addition of pious legend-making, how, they ask, is the plain man to know what is fact and what is fancy?

More difficult still is the question of determining the extent to which Christian belief is dependent upon the findings of historical inquiry. And here the problems crowd in thick and fast. We find ourselves faced with the issues raised by what is generally known as Form-criticism. How far are the Gospels, which earlier generations have taken as more or less straightforward records of the facts of our Lord's life and ministry, to be regarded as such any longer? Are they not more correctly seen as the end-product of years of verbal proclamation of those facts in missionary preaching? And who is to say how much the original may have been elaborated and distorted in that process? Is there any hope of getting behind what is now described as 'the impression left on the mind of the Christian Church by the fact of Jesus' to the fact itself?

There is the demand for 'demythologizing' which is associated with the name of Rudolph Bultmann. And here it is essential to understand the context in which this problem has arisen. Bultmann found himself as an army chaplain faced with the attempt to convey Christian truth to men to whom the whole background and presuppositions of Biblical thought were largely meaningless. It was not for him a question of the *truth* of the Gospel, but of its intelligibility to the contemporary mind. I cannot do better than quote the passage in which Mr Woods describes the situation as Bultmann saw it.

He has no doubt that the New Testament is the proclamation of the Gospel of Salvation. It bears witness to the saving act of God in Christ. Christ is the saving word of God. But for the modern mind, which is deeply influenced by scientific studies and technical progress, the form in which the saving act is presented is largely incredible or incomprehensible. We no longer believe the setting in which the act is said to have taken place, nor can we understand the modes in which the act itself is described. We can believe that the saving act took place, but we no longer believe that it took place as the New Testament relates. We no longer believe that the world is the middle section of a physical universe containing hell beneath and heaven above. It is, therefore, not possible for us to envisage spiritual activity as the movements of spirits from above or below. We do not conceive of spiritual activity as a series of incursions and excursions between spatially contingent realms. The stage setting of the act of salvation which we find in the New Testament is no longer accepted by us as true.

It was to Bultmann intolerable that such a situation should be allowed to continue without action being taken. It is the pastoral duty of those who speak in the name of the Church to make the Gospel known in forms which, while they sacrifice nothing which is essential to the Gospel, raise no *avoidable* rational or moral problems for those to whom they speak. The claim that God acted in Christ to save the world will indeed always remain astounding: but that is no reason why the difficulty should be made greater by the fact that the terms in which the truth is expressed have ceased to be intelligible. When men are failing to recognize and accept the gift of salvation, it is folly to insist on their receiving it in the mental box in which it was originally given.*

There would certainly be many competent scholars who would agree emphatically with Mr Woods's comment that Bultmann exaggerates the extent to which the writings of the New Testament are unintelligible, and underestimates the sustained awareness in Christian history of the limitations of human language in regard to the being and activity of God. And certainly there will be many who find themselves unable to accept the 'existential' solution which he proposes for the difficulty. But no one with any experience of educational or evangelistic work, especially with young people, can fail to

* Woods, *Theological Explanation* (Nisbet, 1958), pp. 198–9.

recognize the reality of the problem which he raises, or to sympathize with his intense desire to meet it even by radical methods of reinterpretation.

Illustrations such as these may serve to indicate the difficulty of the task which confronts the parish priest who seeks to prepare some of his lay people for a ministry of intelligent evangelism. And the problem will not be solved by being tackled only at that level. For clearly the parochial situation points back behind itself to the preparation which is being given to our clergy in their Theological Colleges. This is not the place to embark on anything like a full-scale discussion of this subject, which is, one is thankful to say, receiving pretty searching attention at the moment. But this at least can be said: no man is likely to enter upon his ministry with the outlook and equipment which will enable him to meet its demands, if he has been taught his theology *in a vacuum*. Proper academic teaching and study there must be: and the higher the level of it the better. But it can never be truly *theological*, as the Bible understands that word, unless all the time it is seeking to illustrate the purpose and the working of God in terms of actual history and human situations.

That first. And second: no man will be able to meet the demands of the ministry unless he has received a really adequate grounding at least in the principles and methods of adult education. And that means something much more than technical 'know-how'. It means that he must have had bitten into his soul the conviction that he goes to his work as much a learner as a teacher, ready and anxious to draw out the rich experience which is to be found among many of those to whom he will be ministering, to sit at their feet in the school of life, and often enough in the school of the knowledge of God.

What does it add up to? What has the Spirit to say to a Church grappling with an immensely complex, and an immensely stimulating, intellectual situation?

Perhaps the best answer is to be found in yet another familiar saying from the same source: 'He will take the things which belong to me, and make their meaning plain to you' (John 16:14). This chapter has not been a plea for the invention of a new Gospel to meet the changing conditions of our time. 'Other foundation can no man lay but that which has been laid, even Jesus Christ.' That truth stands firm. But what the Johannine saying indicates is that there is no such thing as 'the faith once delivered to the saints', if by that is meant a nice tidy packet of truth which we can put in our pocket and produce in its wrappings as required. What it does indicate is that the potential meanings and implications of the revelation given in Christ are inexhaustible. But they can only be made known and available to those who are prepared to let the Spirit expose them. And that does not mean sitting with folded hands waiting for inspiration. It means the humble acknowledgement of how little as yet we know of what the Gospel means. It means the zest and inquisitiveness which will set us exploring new lines of inquiry and experiment. It means a lot of darned hard work.

CHAPTER 10

Christian Involvement in Society

FOR everyone who confidently or reluctantly abandons Christian belief because he can no longer regard it as a tenable intellectual option, there are a hundred who, often almost imperceptibly, have ceased to regard that belief as of any practical relevance or importance.

There are the men and women in positions of responsibility at many different levels in business, professional, and civic life. They are personally concerned to maintain standards of integrity and competence. They recognize the vital importance of right human relationships. But to many of them religion appears to have little or nothing to say to the situations, individual and large-scale, in which their problems arise.

Even in the individual sphere Christian ethical guidance appears to be more concerned with the relationships which are to be found inside the family than with those which arise in the factory or the office or the committee room. And on the large-scale, what evidence is there that those who speak in the name of the Church are trying to understand the moral issues which are to be found just below the surface of wage-arbitration, or a change-over in production which may affect the domestic life of large numbers of workers, or the decisions which have to be taken by the Housing Committee or the Health Committee of a local authority? Such things are scarcely mentioned in the sermons, or even in the prayers, at Sunday worship. And if individual members of the congregation seek the counsel of their parish priest as to their Christian duty in such matters, in which they can seldom act solely as individual conscience may dictate, they do not very often find much in the way of understanding.

At a less responsible level, there are thousands to whom religion looks like a comparatively harmless hobby for those who happen to have that peculiar taste. Other people prefer to devote their spare time to pigeon-fancying, or gardening, or music, or hiking, or League football, or even politics. If there are people who are so oddly made that they like going to church, well, it is still a free country. Let them amuse themselves in their own way. But for the majority religion just doesn't register. The spectacular growth of agencies of social responsibility has displaced the pastoral help of the clergy and the official action of Church Societies in meeting many of the accidents and disabilities of daily life. If things go wrong there is a host of competent public bodies which can be relied on to deal with the situation more efficiently. And if now and then men and women find themselves faced with a crisis which touches life more intimately and deeply, the chances are that the psychiatrist or the Child Guidance Clinic, or the Marriage Guidance Council, will be able to cope. Even in the face of death the calling in of the priest is no more than a concession to convention. It is doubtful whether he can give any help that could not equally well be provided by a sympathetic doctor or even a tactful funeral director.

A somewhat one-sided picture, no doubt. But does it not contain sufficient truth to make the temptation to shut our eyes to it a real and dangerous one?

Our business in this chapter is to ask ourselves how a Church which, again, is 'living in the Spirit' will be trying to meet a situation in which for very many religion appears to have lost its hold upon the greater part of their waking and working life; in which, more seriously still, it appears to have no informed comment to make, and no effective contribution to offer, in the realm of political and economic decisions which affect the well-being of the community.

Clearly the first question which we have to face is the basic one of whether this concern with 'this-worldly' affairs, this attempt to bring the Gospel to bear upon political, economic, and social issues *is* the Church's proper business. There are certain types of religious thought which would give a definitely negative answer.

Readers of Dr Vidler's *Christian Belief and this World** will remember the question which he poses in his opening chapter 'Should Christians be Non-conformists?' He is using the word of course not in its ordinary ecclesiastical sense, but as implying detachment from, refusal to be involved in, the affairs of secular life. He marshals the evidence on both sides of the argument. A strong case can be made for the 'non-conformist' view, based on direct evidence from the sayings of Jesus himself, and from the clear fact that many of his followers in this respect took him at his word. There is the argument from Church history which can, not implausibly, be read as supporting the statement that ever since the fatal surrender to the offer of Constantine, 'Christians have throughout the major part of their history been trying to have the best of both worlds, and have in consequence produced a caricature, not to say a flat contradiction, of the discipleship which they have continued to profess.' And for good measure it can be pointed out that many of the significant movements of protest and reformation have been directed precisely against this surrender to 'conformity'.

But a stronger case can be made out on the other side. No one can take the Biblical evidence as a whole without realizing on which side of the question it falls. This is God's world, which he made and saw was good. He loves it in spite of its corruption; his purpose is one of redemption and restoration. And the evidence of the Gospels interpreted at depth clearly points in the same direction. The Parables are supremely significant. To the best of my recollection only one of them is concerned with specifically 'religious' behaviour. All the rest deal with such things as cooking and darning and

* S.C.M., 1956.

housekeeping, and farming and gardening and banking and dealing in precious stones or real estate. They seem to indicate that if you want to estimate the real quality and worth of human life, you look at it in those settings, in work-day dress, not in its best clothes and on its best behaviour on Sunday. And they seem to imply, which is far more significant, that it is in the attitudes of men as seen in their secular occupations – their care of their property, their skill and patience in the treatment of their land and its products – that you get a clue to the kind of trouble which God takes over looking after *his* property, and fostering the growth of *his* crops.

Nor are the arguments from Christian history confined to the support of one side only. Inevitably in the early stages the influence which the Church could exert on the affairs of the world was small; but no one who reflects on the content, for instance, of Paul's letters, or of some of the 'Apologies' of Christian writers in the first few centuries, can fail to recognize in them a sense of deep and serious concern for the responsibilities of Christians in their social environment.

But the decisive point is to ask whether taken literally, in its strict form, the argument for non-involvement does not reduce itself to both a practical and a moral absurdity. 'Are we really expected to believe that God intended all the hard political work, which must be done if tolerable conditions for human existence are to be preserved on the earth, to be done by infidels, if it was to be done at all? Would not that be equivalent to saying that God meant Christians to be parasites on the life of the world at large, to draw their skirts around them so as not to be soiled by its cares and occupations, and to leave other people to do all the dirty work?'*

That stings, and rightly. For there is a real danger of the Church coming to appear, even to be, parasitic upon society. There are not many, maybe, who would put it as bluntly as that. But there are very many who would, if they are honest,

* Op. cit., p. 21.

say that the Church seems to them quite irrelevant, a detached departmental item in the life of the community.

It is of course essential to make sure of the sense in which we are using our words. There is perhaps a danger of confusion and misunderstanding in using the word 'conformity' to indicate involvement or concern. Clearly conformity, in the sense in which the word is commonly used, is something against which the Gospel from the very beginning has uttered the strongest possible warning. And Church history is littered with evidence of the disastrous consequences which have followed from the refusal to heed those warnings. But that is not the sense in which we are considering the question in this chapter. Our argument here is directed against those who, actuated maybe by the fear of the dangers of 'conformity' in its usual sense, deny that the Church is engaged upon its true purpose and mission when it seeks to meet men where they are, caught up in the complex of political, industrial, and social undertakings, and to make its presentation of the Gospel such as will speak to them *in those conditions*, and to the conditions themselves. With that view there can, in my judgement, be no truce.

In *Church and People in an Industrial City* * Canon (now Bishop) Wickham has rendered an immense service to the whole Church. On the basis of a detailed survey of the record of the Anglican and Free Churches in Sheffield over the past one and a half centuries, he has exposed the situation with which we find ourselves confronted today. And he has done it with brutal honesty. The details may differ somewhat from area to area. Bristol certainly presents a rather different picture from Sheffield. But by and large it is the same throughout the industrial life of our country. The Churches have little effective contact with the life of the workers. It is doubtful whether they possess their respect and affection. And within the last fifty years there has been an appreciable weakening of the

* Lutterworth, 1957.

allegiance of the managerial and executive sections of industry, on which, in the latter half of the nineteenth century, they could count to a considerable extent.

It is in the concluding chapter, 'Mission of the Church in an Industrial Society', that we come face to face with the issue which we are considering in this closing section: What is the Spirit of God saying to the Churches in face of, in terms of, the actual human needs which are being created by the pressures, cultural and economic, of our time?

If I read Canon Wickham's conclusions aright, his answer to this question falls under three main heads. There is need for (1) vigorous theological thinking, (2) experiments of many kinds in what he calls 'Industrial Mission', and (3) a radical rethinking of the traditional parochial pattern.

Let us first consider theological thinking. Here we have got to get down to the roots and ask the fundamental question: What is the true relation of the Church to society? There are those who would answer that question by setting before us the ideal of the Church as utterly apart, a 'fenced city', an Ark of Salvation amid the flood. There are others who would still advocate the idea of a 'national' Church, in the sense of an organ of a community still regarded as Christian, or at least potentially Christian.

Neither of these alternatives is acceptable. The first amounts to surrender, a retreat to the catacombs. There may indeed be situations in the life of a nation in which the pressures of opposition or persecution are so strong that there is no other possible line of action to be taken. But that is not the situation which confronts the Churches in England at the present time. The position is still, thank God, far more open to positive lines of action. Indeed there is plenty of evidence that this 'last ditch' policy is exactly what does not commend itself to those who are still our allies and would-be cooperators in the world of business and politics.

The second is certainly more congenial to the temper of our

national history, and indeed it contains elements of truth which no thoughtful man would willingly surrender. But it has to be judged by hard facts. And in the opinion of many, those facts strain its claim to realism to the limit. At the parochial level the debate between the advocates of 'rigorist' and 'liberal' strategies in dealing, for instance, with the pastoral demands of a housing-estate will doubtless continue. And it is certainly wholesome that it should. We shall do well to preserve and foster any opportunities which are still honestly afforded us to remind men that 'the Church reflects the total life of the Christian community' as a means to encouraging the community to feel that it 'embodies in its life the insights and valuations of Christian faith'. But we must be constantly on our guard against allowing a nostalgic desire to retain this 'co-inherence' to blind us to the danger that it can degenerate into 'conformity' in the worst sense, in which the religious pattern has become nothing more than a veneer upon a culture and social life which are no longer informed by its faith.

But we are not shut in to a choice between these two alternative interpretations of the function of the Church. It is possible to think of the Church as a society which is indeed distinguished and distinct from the world around it by the belief on which it lives, and by the dynamic with which that belief inspires the life and conduct of its members, but which is all the time seeking to work out the meaning of its belief, and the practical consequences of it in terms of the secular world to which its members belong. Such a view does indeed demand as its means of expression a close and continuous 'involvement' in the affairs of communal life. 'It roots Christian obedience in the world, from which it so easily escapes into "religion", and it demands that Christian men seek God's will for the world, with which the Christian faith is seen to be patently concerned. The hard facts of a scientific and technological organization of society, and the welter of social revolution the world over, can then be seen not as awkward difficulties which it must somehow live with, but as the raw material out of which our age has to be built, and through which the living God confronts our century.'*

Here indeed is a call to radical theological thinking. Here indeed is a sphere in which we may call upon the Spirit 'to lead us into the totality of truth'. For there will be a deal of hard graft to be done in putting ourselves to school with those who can enlighten us from inside as to some of the strains and stresses to which human nature is exposed in living in such a society as ours, who can help us to understand at even greater depth the modern 'principalities and powers', the pervasive and dominating factors in our civilization which can enslave or liberate men, stunt or increase their stature as men. These 'principalities and powers' matter at least as much as the 'flesh and blood' of ordinary pastoral ministration.

Equally of course we must invoke the illumination of the Spirit in 'taking the things which belong to Christ and making their meaning plain to us'. For nothing less than that will meet the need. There is no question here of thinking up some newfangled Gospel which will satisfy the demands of 'technological man'. There may well be in Dietrich Bonhoeffer's† famous hint, a need to think out means by which we can communicate the Gospel to those for whom 'religion' has become almost an impossibility, to ask ourselves 'how we speak of God in secular terms, and how Christ can be Lord of those without religion'. But it must be of God and of Christ that we speak. And it is the Spirit 'who proceeds from the Father and the Son' who must teach us.

Industrial Mission and the rethinking of the traditional parochial system: these two inevitably go together. They are not mutually exclusive alternatives. They are essentially

* Op. cit., p. 234. The preceding paragraphs owe much to a review by the Archbishop of York of Canon Wickham's work.

† *Letters and Papers from Prison* (S.C.M., 1933), pp. 122 f.

related parts of a strategy which seeks to use the Church's experience and resources in ways which will meet a rapidly changing situation. Nothing is more common, or more unfortunate, than to set the two over against one another as contradictory or even antagonistic methods of work.

The radical theological thinking is necessary, but it cannot stand alone. Indeed the history of the last half-century provides more than enough evidence that top-level attempts to re-present the Christian Gospel in the kind of terms which have been suggested in preceding paragraphs may produce little lasting effect. They make no direct impact upon industrial life; nor do they necessarily produce closer and more sympathetic relations between those concerned in it and the representatives of the Church.

It needs to be supplemented by a carefully planned and consistently sustained development of personal relationships. I have the right to speak only from the angle of the Church of England; but personal acquaintance with a good many Free Churchmen would lead me to believe that their experience would bear out what has been my own. The fact is that the Church must win the right to make any such contribution to industrial life as is here suggested by regaining the trust and respect of those who direct and work in it. And that can only be done by an approach, at once humble and honest. We have to confess past failure and neglect. We have to acknowledge that we are in the main ignorant of much that we ought to know, since it vitally concerns the personal well-being and happiness of thousands of the men and women to whom we are supposed to minister. We have to make a frank appeal to the men, at all levels, who hold the keys of entry in their hands to open the doors and let us in.

In some cases these doors are literally the doors of factories and shops and offices. For under certain conditions it is certainly possible to carry out this work of reconnaissance and establishing contact by direct entry to the board-room and the shop-floor. But it is by no means always true that this is the best way to start, or that in the circumstances of a particular locality it will ever become the most effective means of communication. In any case there is always a vast deal of quiet unobtrusive work to be done behind the scenes by consultation with small groups of men who represent the diverse interests and levels of authority. And that can often better be done at times and in places which raise no possibility of trespassing or of interference with regulations.

How is such work to be inaugurated, and by whom is it to be carried on? Canon Wickham makes a strong plea for the inclusion in the Church's strategy of a top-level national approach, since in his judgement nothing more local or restricted than this can meet the needs of the ever larger groupings and more widespread ramifications of the big industries. I have little experience of this aspect of the undertaking; but it is obvious that some organs of consultation which can rightly be regarded as expressing the mind of the Church as a whole are essential. Needless to say, he does not ignore the more localized experiment. And indeed it is clear to anyone who knows the Sheffield experiment that it is only on the basis of knowledge and trust acquired in a number of local situations that any national policy can be developed.

Given the right approach, there is no question that a response will be forthcoming. Indeed before very long the problem becomes one of keeping abreast of all the openings which present themselves. It becomes apparent that only a *group* of men carefully selected and trained for the purpose can consolidate the position and develop further lines of experiment.

But – and again it is a large but – no such approach, and no such expansion, will really be effective, unless it is seen and felt by all concerned to be indeed expressive of the conviction and the desire of the *whole* Church in the city or neighbourhood.

And here we find ourselves facing the other half of the practical task. This kind of frontier work is only too likely to remain detached and isolated unless it is reinforced by the sympathetic understanding and cooperation of the men who are responsible at the parochial end for the pastoral care of the homes in which those who work in industry live.

If this is to be forthcoming, certain conditions must be fulfilled. The first and most obvious is the learning by all concerned of that elementary truth which Paul so constantly reaffirms. 'There are diversities of gifts, but the same Spirit: all of them are the work of the one self-same Spirit who distributes to each individually as he sees fit.' The parochial system has been an immense source of strength to the Church of England. What would not the Communist Party give for such a set-up? The work of the parochial clergy is, in the majority of cases at the present time, beyond all praise for its unselfish devotion. But there is no escaping the fact that too exclusive a reliance on this one method has produced a limited outlook, and even a 'parochial' jealousy, which is today a grave obstacle to the deploying of the Church's strength on new fronts.

There would, I believe, be few better ways of breaking down this isolation, and the temper which it tends to breed, than the fostering in parish priests of the realization that their work is one aspect of an over-all pastoral and evangelistic effort which seeks to reach men and women by a variety of approaches, of which Industrial Mission is one.

But there is more to it than this. The restrictedness of outlook is not purely geographical or even functional. It affects men's understanding of their work at a deeper level. Let me put it rather crudely. If a man attends church regularly over a period of time, what impression is he likely to form of the subjects in which the Church appears to be interested? 'Religion', worship, prayer, Bible study, sacramental life; personal character widening out into the sphere

of personal relationships in the family and among neighbours; an occasional reference to religious education; and –
separated by a wide interval – Foreign Missions, the work
of the Church overseas. Yes, I know it is crude, and in some
cases quite unjust. But in the main, is it not true that if men
stopped to think about it, they would become conscious of
an immense gap, a gap which is filled by most of what happens
between clocking-in and clocking-out on five days in the
week?

How can Christian faith, so presented, come home to people
as a Gospel for the whole of life, as speaking to them at just
those points, in just those situations, where they are often
most conscious of the need for moral reinforcement?

After twelve years' experience at close quarters of the work
of the parochial clergy, I realize full well what is likely to be
the reaction of the best of them to the suggestion that there is
a considerable area of responsibility which is being largely
neglected! Fortunately, I believe that I know the answer.

A very large part of what is required will not fall on their
shoulders. There *will* be a distinctive and vital contribution
which they must make, but the bulk of the work must be
undertaken by the laity: by the men and women who already
are the Church in the setting of working life. For the clergy
it will not mean the addition of another large item to an
already over-full programme. It *will* mean the adjustment
of the existing items in that programme to make room for
something which, rightly understood, must surely rank high
on any list of priorities, and which, I can assure them, will
prove to be one of the most rewarding of their tasks.

In every urban or residential parish there will be members
of the congregation, not to mention fringers, who are earning
their living in factories, shops, offices, social service, local
government. These people are the potential of the Church's
impact on that world. They will need to be gathered together
and helped to see that this is what they are, that it is in this

sphere that their 'vocation and ministry' lie. And they will need to be trained.

That training is a two-way traffic. They themselves must supply a large part of the evidence on which any effective course of training will depend. What are their needs? Where does the shoe pinch in their job? What are the points at which they are already conscious of conflict and tension between existing practices and what they know, even if rather inarticulately, to be the standards which Christians should be trying to set?

Then, and only then, we turn to our Bibles, to the great affirmations of Christian faith and ask what light these have to throw upon the actual situations laid bare by the honest assessment which has already taken place. There will be questions of individual conduct, and of business ethics. But deeper still there will be far-reaching questions of the Christian view of *work as such*. Why do men work, and why ought they to work? What makes men like and respect or dislike and despise it? What is the true relation of *making*, of production, to *getting*, the pay packet? By what means can Christians, individually or collectively, bring an influence to bear upon situations and practices which they see to be a contradiction of the clear deliverances of their faith about God and man?

It is a tremendous undertaking; and for the most part it is unexplored territory. But therein lie its challenge and stimulus. Here indeed is the chance for the Spirit to open our eyes to new ventures of understanding and experiment. Here indeed is the opportunity to discover that this old faith which we have tended to think of as something confined to, I had almost said buried in, Bible and Creeds, is coming alive with astonishing relevance to actual contemporary situations.

Nor is it only on the intellectual plane that the distinctive influence of the Spirit will be needed. We need to remind ourselves yet once again that his most characteristic operation is the creation of fellowship. And nowhere is that task more beset with difficulty than in the bridging of the gap between representatives of the Church in an official sense and those who represent a world in which the Church appears to have shown little or no interest for so long.

There will be a deal of suspicion and resistance to be overcome. There will have to be genuine expression of penitence for long years of apathy and apparent toleration of social injustice. There will have to be a lot of listening and learning before there is much in the way of counsel or guidance. Above all there will have to be a deliberate repudiation of any suggestion that the Church's aim in this approach to those who for the most part have lost any connexion with Church membership is the production of 'pew-fodder'. We may indeed believe that reintegration in the life of a worshipping community is the only means by which in the end men's spiritual need can be satisfied. But it will take a long time to bring that conviction home to many of those to whom we speak. And it will be fatal to present that conviction until a very great deal has been done to awaken in them the realization that in the last resort their need is spiritual, *and* so to transform much of the worship and life of the Church that it can truly vindicate its claim to satisfy such a need.

I have illustrated this issue of the Church's involvement with the world from the sphere of industry and business. But precisely the same point could have been made with reference to such spheres as the social services or local government.

In the case of the former the demand could indeed have been put much more strongly. For very many of the admirable agencies which now provide a network of research, supervision, financial assistance, and personal care in the fields of health and welfare are the direct inheritors of the Church's initiative and charity. What is more, in many cases they are staffed by men and women who are themselves deeply inspired by a sense of Christian vocation, and draw not a little of the patience and wisdom and generosity which characterize their work from a direct Christian source.

How much more could they draw, and how much more fruitful the relationship between them and the Church could be, if the Church were more intelligently and sympathetically aware of the potential partnership, and made it more plain that their work is quite definitely regarded as an expansion of the Church's mission.

That there are obstacles to be overcome here is clear enough. As in the sphere of education, so in the sphere of social service it is not always easy for those who in the past have occupied a position of ownership, control, and authority to accept a radical shift of balance and learn a new technique of partnership. And on the other side, a new-found independence, professional and financial, is apt to produce for a time at least an attitude of detachment from, and even contempt for, 'amateur' efforts which can no longer compete in technical efficiency.

But the possibility and the need are there. And there could be few better opportunities for affirming and discovering the work of God's Spirit beyond the bounds of 'Church' life. It would mean an immense expansion of our far too restricted idea of 'evangelism'. Equally it would preserve, or even introduce, within the social services an element for which one may perhaps borrow a phrase from Professor Dorothy Emmet, the element of 'charismatic personality', that indefinable quality which shows itself when the service of humanity draws its inspiration from the love of God.

There remains another sphere in which the same work of integration must be attempted, the sphere of politics. It is, I think, definitely the most difficult of the three. In industrial and business life the element of personal relationship and responsibility is unmistakably present, even when the growth in size and complexity of many such undertakings makes the exercise of it increasingly harder. In the social services the same thing is true, though here again the supersession of voluntary agencies by omnicompetent state organization may easily lead to the ignoring of the personal equation. In both these cases, however, it is still possible to see and assert a Christian implication in the aim and character of the work itself.

It is not easy to claim as much for politics, at least on the national scale. It may well be the fact that there are today more committed Christians among the members of our legislative assemblies than at some previous periods of history. But they themselves, I fancy, would be the first to confess that the extent to which their Christian commitment can translate itself into effective action in terms of parliamentary procedure appears very uncertain. Only very occasionally it would seem do issues arise in which a clear non-partisan expression of Christian ethical judgement can be made.

In the sphere of local politics the situation is appreciably different. No one who has observed with any close attention the working of local government in a big city can be in any doubt that here indeed is a situation which offers an immensely valuable opportunity for the exercise of Christian responsibility and service.

It is an opportunity which presents itself in a variety of forms. The members of a City Council, and its committees, are men and women who have voluntarily put their time and abilities at the disposal of the community, and have been entrusted by it with the discharge of duties which at a dozen different points vitally affect the well-being, physical, mental, and moral, of their fellow-citizens. How many of our Church people have seriously faced the question whether they ought not to offer themselves, if suitably qualified, for such service? How many of them have been encouraged to do so by their clergy? Is it not at least as likely that they have been discouraged from any such idea, because election would mean that they would no longer be available to the same extent for 'church-work'?

Some of them, thank God, do take the plunge. But when they do, and have, maybe, reached a post of responsibility in the departments of education, health, housing, or finance, which gives them a real opportunity to exercise an effective Christian influence, they find to their dismay that so far as they can see the Church as a whole, even sometimes their own congregation, appears to be completely indifferent to the problems which, as churchmen, they are facing, and affords little or nothing in the way of spiritual support. Their work seldom finds a place among the regular subjects for intercession in public worship. It never seems to have occurred to the congregation, or the parish priest, that opportunities might be provided for them to speak to a parish meeting about the issues with which they are concerned week in, week out. I well remember one such, outstanding alike in his professional work and as an effective servant of his Church, remarking to me, 'You know, Bishop, I've been in local government now for something like ten years; and the only occasion on which I have received any approach or representation from Christians was when the issue of the Sunday opening of cinemas was coming up.' Could there be a more damning exposure of the narrowness of our understanding of the true nature of the Church's responsibility to the community? Actual participation in local government as a Councillor is obviously only possible for a very small minority. Informed interest in, and active support of, their work is the responsibility of every member of the Church.

CHAPTER 11

The Recovery of Unity

WE have considered in the preceding chapters two of the spheres in which a Church which is really seeking to live in the Spirit may expect to find new inspiration and power at work, opening its eyes to new demands and possibilities, and supplying the dynamic with which to meet them.

There is the challenge once more to vindicate the truth of the Christian view of man's life against new philosophies which offer rival interpretations. Or to put it, as I think, more accurately and justly, to examine these in order to detect where they themselves contain insights into truth which, because they are the prompting of God's Spirit, need to be taken into account and incorporated in a fresh formulation of faith.

There is the challenge to demonstrate that this faith is one which takes into its purview the *whole* of human life, which realizes that 'the Reign of God' is the vision not of some ecclesiastical enclave but of an order of human society, in which God's writ runs and his will is done throughout the whole structure.

And as we face these two tasks we become painfully conscious of a question which stands over against us and demands to be answered before much real progress can be made with the others. Can a Church, which by its disunity is patently denying the express will of its master, expect or hope to be able to convince the world of the truth of its Gospel or demonstrate that the way of life which it sets forth is the answer to its need? That blunt proverb 'Physician, heal thyself' needs to be writ large across the front page of every 'restatement of the faith' or 'programme of social action'. We forget at our peril that *the* distinctive gift of the Spirit in the New Testament is 'unity, in the bond of peace'.

When the history of the Church in the twentieth century comes to be written, its outstanding characteristic will, beyond any question, be the movement towards the recovery of unity which began in the first decade and shows signs of continuing with gathering momentum and effectiveness.

Chapter 10 of *A History of the Oecumenical Movement** is entitled 'Plans of Union and Reunion'. It is followed by an appendix which contains a complete list of all the negotiations which have taken place between separated Churches in the years 1910–52. The list contains ninety-one entries. The page headings of the appendix tell in a revealing way the story of the very various types of negotiation, and of the measure of success or otherwise which had up to that date attended them: 'Bone to his Bone', 'Across Confessional Boundaries', 'Intercommunion without Union', 'Without Loss of Sovereignty', 'Hopes for the Future', 'Hope not untempered by Anxiety', 'Cold Storage', 'But perhaps not for ever'.

Many of the actual unions achieved have been between Churches within the same Confession, divided by something less than fundamental doctrinal principles. Notable here are the unions between the Church of Scotland and the United Free Church of Scotland, and between the Wesleyan, United, and Primitive Methodists.

Others, described as 'trans-confessional', include the United Church of North India and the United Church of Canada. Neither of these involves union between Episcopal and non-Episcopal Churches. That great achievement has been realized only by the Church of South India.

Other projects of the same kind are on foot, at one or another stage of progress. The plans for union (on analogous lines to South India) in North India and Pakistan, and in

* Ruth Rouse and S. C. Neill (S.P.C.K., 1954).

Ceylon, are far advanced. Signs of the same kind of movement can be detected in Nigeria.

And alongside these are a variety of movements which have achieved or are aiming at a Federal relationship, full or partial Intercommunion; and at a still earlier stage, 'Conversations', as between the Church of England and the Methodist Church, or the two Episcopal and Presbyterian Churches of England and Scotland.

A perplexing list to the outside observer; an excuse maybe for sardonic comment by the cynic, not least when he notices that a number of the negotiations have been 'discontinued'; certainly a ground for shame to the Christian when he counts the full tale of the separated bodies; and yet, when one realizes that all this has happened within the space of less than fifty years, and that within the previous two or three centuries little or nothing of the kind had happened, a cause for profound thankfulness.

The mere list of achievements is sufficiently impressive. But impressive as it is, it cannot by itself convey the inner significance of what has happened as the result of all these years spent in discussion and argument.

The representatives of Churches which have been separated from any effective contact with one another, from anything between two hundred and four hundred years, have discovered that despite this they are still in agreement on by far the greater part of the content of the Creed. It is true that different emphases are undoubtedly to be found in the interpretation of even the central affirmations of the faith. But they are not differences which in the main run along denominational lines: they cut clean across these frontiers, and are much more likely to align themselves with age-groups, or geographical or cultural backgrounds. There is no distinctive Anglican doctrine of the Incarnation, or Methodist doctrine of the Atonement, or Presbyterian doctrine of Eternal Life. The area of real divergence is in the main confined to beliefs about the nature of the Church, the Ministry, and the Sacraments. Here indeed is a point the significance of which we shall have to explore further at a later stage. But for the moment we can thankfully register the fact that the Spirit, who is the Spirit of truth, has made it possible for divided, and often quarrelling, Churches to hold fast to the essentials of a common faith to a degree which, when they do begin to meet one another again, enables them to register an astonishing amount of mutual agreement. And for chapter and verse, here is the official statement from the Interim Report (1949) of the Conversations between representatives of the Church of England and the Free Churches:

> On the doctrines of God the Father, the Person and Work of Christ, the Person and Mission of the Holy Spirit, the Trinity, and the Life Everlasting we have found nothing which separates any one of these Communions from one another. All acknowledge the Apostolic faith as contained in the Scriptures and expressed in the Apostles' and Nicene Creeds.

('Then why in the name of fortune', comments the plain man, 'don't they unite?' Why indeed!)

A second discovery is of almost equal importance. Psychology has familiarized us with the fact that it is by no means always easy to identify and acknowledge the real motives on which we are acting. Unconscious 'rationalization' is never far round the corner. In the case of the movement towards unity, it is natural that all of us should like to believe that the grounds on which we feel that we must maintain our distinctive Church positions, are grounds of high doctrinal principle. These we must stand for: to surrender them would mean an offence against conscience, the betrayal of a sacred trust committed to us.

Of course there is a measure of truth in this. But it is by no means the whole story. The point is well put by Professor C. H. Dodd in his contribution to the pamphlet 'Social and Cultural Factors in Church Divisions'.*

* S.C.M. Press, 1951.

In the course of nearly forty years' participation in conferences and discussion having reunion as their ultimate aim, I have often been puzzled by a recurrent phenomenon. When certain issues have been patiently thrashed out, and we have come, through a deeper mutual understanding, within sight of some real measure of agreement on those particular issues, suddenly the ground of debate shifts. Some fresh point of division emerges, which no one had spoken about, or thought about, much. Interest in the matters hitherto under discussion evaporates, and the measure of agreement attained appears quite insignificant. We are thrown back to the beginning. Sometimes such a throw-back has proved salutary, because we have been neglecting some genuine point of misunderstanding. ... But I am sure it has not always been so. The throw-back is not always a case of *reculer pour mieux sauter*. It means that we are shying at the logical consequences of steps we felt bound to take, and we are now casting about for good reasons why we should not follow out these consequences. But the real reasons may be avowed or subconscious.

They may indeed. And we do well to keep a watchful eye on the possibility of such self-deception.

But even when we are on our guard against this subtle danger, there are other possible misreadings of the facts which can be a serious cause of obstruction to effective progress. A later essay in that same pamphlet, 'Non-Theological Factors Causing and Perpetuating Divisions', exposes a number of other influences which can operate to heighten, and even to distort, genuine theological divergences.

Churches or groups of Churches have grown up, maybe for centuries, in geographical or cultural separation from one another. Their respective traditions of faith and worship are interwoven with alien patterns of social, even political, life which they do not willingly change or surrender in the cause of unity. Even where separated Churches have been living in close contiguity, they may well have been in the main representative of different social or economic strata in the life of the one community. No one who can recall the cleavage between

'Church of England' and 'Dissenters' in village life fifty years
ago will need to be reminded that the forces of segregation
were at least as much social and economic as theological!
There have been historical influences at work in the shape
of victimization or persecution of a minority by a majority.
Even where the pressure may not have gone that length, there
may have been social or racial discrimination. There have
been ejections and secessions of groups of 'reformers' or 're-
vivalists', who found themselves unable to express the truth
as they saw it or to follow the forms of worship which satisfied their spiritual needs, within the limits of the Church to
which they originally belonged. Even union movements
themselves have been the cause of fresh formations of dis-
sident 'splinter groups'. And in all these cases sociological
and psychological reasons, possibly even the ambition or
bigotry of dominant personalities, have played a not incon-
siderable part.

So long as Churches kept at arm's length, it was likely
enough that factors such as these might remain undetected.
It has been one of the great gains of getting to grips with one
another in frank and sustained discussion, that many of them
have been brought out into the open. The acknowledgement,
often by both sides, that their mistrust of one another was
not solely due to suspicion of doubtful orthodoxy, has had a
salutary effect.

But perhaps the greatest single advance is the new realization of the true presupposition from which, if any real progress
is to be made, all our discussions must start. A quotation from
the Report *Church Relations in England* will bring out the significance of this point:

So long as our divisions persist, a modern 'Church' could only
claim to correspond to that of the New Testament on the hypothesis
that it alone is the true Church. This would seem to be the position
of the Eastern Orthodox and the Roman Catholic Churches. On
that view all other Christian bodies, whether heretical, or orthodox

but schismatic, are outside the Church. None of the Churches represented among us (Anglican, Baptist, Congregational, Methodist, Moravian, Presbyterian, Churches of Christ) takes up this position.

Instead they make the acknowledgement that all alike are involved in a situation which has been described as '*internal schism*'. The implication of that is the recognition that all these Churches are, *by the very fact of division*, imperfect representations of the true Church. The degree of imperfection may differ. Some may have preserved more, others less, of this or that essential element in a truly 'catholic' tradition. But all are involved in the common impoverishment and distortion which springs from division. All acknowledge that they need the contribution which others can supply. All confess that they stand under the common judgement of God, and that they need one another's forgiveness for the sins which have brought them to this state.

This is, to my mind, a step forward of incalculable moral and spiritual importance. It may well be asked why, if so much has been accepted as common ground, advance towards full recognition of one another and full union cannot proceed at a steady, if not a rapid, pace. The answer is to be found of course in the fact that there is still an appreciable area within which no real agreement has been reached.

And here we reach what appears to be the crux of the whole position, the relation of 'Faith' to 'Order'. It is an issue on which perhaps more time and study and discussion have been expended in inter-Church negotiations than on any other. And still there are wide differences of conviction. It is easy – and foolish – to oversimplify issues which wise and good men find to be of the greatest complexity. But it is also permissible to recall the pungent saying of one of the shrewdest critics of the Church, that 'theologians take a perverse delight in making simple issues complicated in order that they may have the satisfaction of demonstrating that they are the only people who are clever enough to sort them out.'

I do not believe that it unfairly oversimplifies the problem to state it thus. All the Christian Churches which are engaged in active and constructive search for the way to unity are agreed that there are certain essential conditions which must be fulfilled in any Church claiming to be regarded as in the historic Christian tradition. They are: the acceptance of the Holy Scriptures, and of the Creeds as the formulations of faith which contain the essentials of the Biblical revelation; the proper administration of the sacraments of Baptism and the Lord's Supper; and a Church Order which carries authority in the matter of faith and discipline.

On the first three of these, there is little or no disagreement among the main Churches of Christendom. On the last, there is agreement as to the necessity of Order as such. Disagreement arises as to the nature of the Order.

I write as an Anglican who deeply values the tradition and heritage of his Church. I am wholly convinced that a due observance of 'Order' has its essential place among the marks of a Church; as I have already said, I believe that a 'religion of the Spirit', if by that is meant the attempt to maintain and propagate a faith, without regard for the institutions by which the corporate life of any body preserves itself in being, is an illusion. Further I believe that, with all its shortcomings past and present, Episcopal Order rightly understood and used has a pastoral contribution of immense value to make to the life of a reunited Church. And there is good evidence for saying that many members of the non-Episcopal Churches would be ready to recognize this, and accept modifications of their own systems such as might make room for episcopacy purged of the manifest and acknowledged defects of its history.

But I recognize also that other Churches have their 'Arks of the Covenant'. They possess Orders, and ministries existing under them, which have in their experience been beyond all question blessed and used by God. And they cannot in conscience accept a method of achieving unity which in their judgement casts a doubt or a slur upon that fact. They claim that they too have a contribution to bring to a reunited Church through the history of their order of ministry.

At this point, over and over again, we reach what appears to be an impasse. Neither side will yield. Neither will accept a transaction which by implication involves some measure of repudiation of their past. I cannot resist the conviction in my own soul that at this point progress is barred not by a principle which stands in equal right with the faith which Christians have received from their Lord, and with the Sacraments of his institution, but by a refusal to accept and follow out the logic of a moral conviction which we have already acknowledged in our recognition of 'internal schism'. Have we not got to say to one another: 'We have all received at God's hands a gift of ministry which has been the source of blessing to our Church. But we have all sinned; and the result of our sin is our divided state. Because of our division none of our ministries, as it stands, can be the universally acknowledged and accepted ministry of a reunited Church. God alone knows what precisely each of our ministries lacks, and what each has to convey to the other. We therefore put the issue in his hands and ask him to use our act of Unification, with the mutual laying on of hands, to give to each order that which in his sight it needs to become part of the universal ministry of his Church.' That would be, as I see it, to trust the Spirit of God instead of attempting to dictate terms to him, which is the one thing above all others which the New Testament makes it plain that we are not to do.

I am well aware that such a mutual acknowledgement would not solve all the problems. We should still be left with the task of thinking out, and working out by experiment, the shape of ministry in a reunited Church which would best express that which each Church has received from God through its traditional pattern of Order. But to make this acknowledgement would, I believe, put us in a position in which the practical task could be undertaken in a spirit which would offer real hope of success, *because* we had got out of our system the virus of denominational pride and insistence on rights. So long as men are saying (under their breath), 'No Bishops at any price', or 'We'll jolly well see that these Methodists get Episcopal ordination, whatever they think they are getting' – and one has heard both things said – there is no hope of any of us being 'led by the Spirit'.

The reader who happens to recall the original instruction mentioned in the Introduction that this was to be a 'non-theological' book, may be pardoned for wondering whether at least it is not becoming somewhat over-ecclesiastical. To which this may be said in reply. No Christian who takes history seriously, who believes that God has been at work in the development of the Church's life through the centuries, using even the sins and blindness of men as the raw material of his purpose, can suppose that we can just wipe out or ignore the record of the past and start with a clean sheet. Unless we understand the causes which have produced our present situation, we cannot hope to remedy the mistakes. And that must be the work of scholars, historians, theologians, liturgiologists. It is highly technical work, calling for infinite patience. And it is safe to say that in every Communion, including some of those which seem outwardly to stand aloof from the Oecumenical Movement, that work is being undertaken with unremitting energy.

But let nobody imagine for a moment that such work by itself will achieve the desired end. Indeed the real trouble is that in every Church there is a handful of leaders who, just because they have devoted time and thought to these issues, are far ahead of the rank and file, and find their work hampered and frustrated by the fact that so few of those whom they represent appear to be remotely interested in or concerned about what they are trying to do. The really remarkable advances towards unity which have been achieved in the last fifty years have been achieved *not* as the result of a surge of prayer and desire throughout the Churches, but in the teeth of ignorance, apathy, and even opposition. 'We don't want to join up with that lot. We're quite content as we are. Leave us alone.'

That at least is true of large sections of the older Churches in the West. Among the younger Churches of Asia and Africa it is, thank God, somewhat different. They are living in situations in which, just because the Christian Church is all the time facing the realities of its mission, they cannot escape for a moment from the disastrous consequences of disunion. The single greatest spiritual advance of our time, the *only* achievement of organic union between Churches of the Catholic and Protestant tradition, in the Church of South India, was made possible because those who were responsible knew that it was impossible for their Churches to do the work to which God had called them while they remained divided. What was the use of preaching a Gospel of reconciliation in Christ, of claiming that the Christian faith was the truth of God for all men, when the retort was so painfully obvious? No one would claim that in South India the rank and file were at the outset enthusiastically eager for such a move. The fact remains that it was because men saw that without it the Church must remain at once impotent and disobedient to God's will, that they were able to overcome doubt and fear and apathy.

The example of South India has kindled the flame elsewhere. No one who was present at the Lambeth Conference in 1958 could mistake the determination of those who spoke for similar schemes in North India and Pakistan, or Ceylon, to carry them through. And what is already clear in India is beginning to become clear in West Africa. The Christians of Asia and Africa readily and gratefully acknowledge that they owe their faith to the Churches of the West. That faith they mean to preserve. What they do *not* want to preserve is a legacy of division, the historical causes of which mean nothing to them, the justification for which they regard as largely outlived.

The question is how long will it be before the Churches in this country wake up to the realization that our situation is not so different from that in the Church overseas? Indeed it is in some ways more serious. There are still parts of Asia and Africa in which the Gospel when it is proclaimed comes as good *news*. It brings a message of the love and power of God which familiarity has not yet staled. Here, as we know only too well, the reception of the preaching may only too likely be: 'That old stuff: we've had that!' But in any case we in this country are faced with the same fact that in any effective sense Christianity is now a minority religion. It is not yet fighting for its life, as it has had to do in some parts of Europe. That might indeed be a blessing. Its situation is more nearly one of dying of inanition. And one at least of the reasons for its loss of appeal and inspiration, especially to the younger generation, is beyond all question its apparent unwillingness to grasp the nettle of disunion. If we ourselves were not blinded by familiarity with our situation, we should realize with horror that many young people are on the way to being excommunicated, because they neither understand nor tolerate the impossibility (in the main due to Anglican prohibition) of meeting with their fellow-Christians in the Sacrament of unity.

How many of us realize that, as in a non-Christian country, so here it is impossible for a divided Church to fulfil its real mission? It can of course go on maintaining the life of parishes and congregations with a fair measure of success. It can point, in not a few cases, to some expansion and increase of numbers. But when it comes to a question of getting out on to the frontier, breaking fresh ground in one or another of those great territories in which so much of the formative work of society is done – education, industry, the social services – we are, whether we are conscious of it or not, disastrously handicapped by the fact that we cannot speak with one voice or present a concerted Christian case.

Why is the rate of progress towards the reunion of the Church so slow? Why has it taken two, three, four centuries for us to set about it at all in real earnest? Why, even now, do we find it so difficult to overcome obstacles which many want to overcome? Why is the main body of Christians in all our Churches pretty nearly a dead weight?

If our study of the New Testament in the earlier chapters was well directed, the answer does not seem far to seek. Over and over again in the speeches which are made in official Church gatherings when the findings of some oecumenical conversation or conference are being discussed, the same phrase recurs: 'Clearly these are very important issues. We must give them the most careful consideration under the guidance of the Holy Spirit.' Is it merely cynical to suspect a mental reservation to the effect that we had better watch very carefully to see that the Spirit does not go too fast? From that disconcerting day at Caesarea (Acts 10), when he upset all the orthodox preconceptions as to the proper order of procedure, there has been the lurking fear in the mind of the Church that really to trust, to commit ourselves to, the Spirit's guidance may be a costly and even dangerous undertaking. And over and over again we have felt that it would be prudent to set him terms, to give him a clearly defined assignment, to make sure that he knows in advance how far we shall be able to follow his guidance.

That comes perilously near the sin which is pilloried throughout the Biblical record of Jewish history, and is finally repudiated in the second of our Lord's temptations, the sin of 'God-tempting'. It takes various forms, but its basic character is always the same. It consists in the attempt to bargain with God, to think that we are in a position to set terms to him, to tell him what we think he should do, and to make our faith in him, our loyalty to him, dependent on his fulfilment of the terms set him.

I would not suggest that when we speak of following the Spirit's guidance we are consciously committing this blasphemy. But it is difficult to resist the impression that we easily allow ourselves to be deceived by the strength of our entrenched Church prejudices and preferences. This is the kind of ecclesiastical setting in which we have grown up; these are the forms and traditions to which we are accustomed; we have been taught to love and revere them; we do not relish the prospect of any major change in them, such as might be required if we were called on to adjust ourselves to the pattern of another Church's life and worship. And because we have through them indeed received God's grace, and grown in our Christian life, we almost automatically assume that they are pleasing to God and that he would not want to see them changed either. That is very nearly to invert the order of faith which the Creed lays down, to make God in the Church's image rather than the reverse. It is at least to reduce to a minimum the place which we assign to the continuing activity of his Spirit.

In the last resort the issue resolves itself into the question of whether all our Churches are prepared to recognize and accept that deepest of all insights into spiritual truth which is enshrined in that passage in John 12:20 ff.

There were some Greeks among those who had come up to worship at the feast. They came to Philip, whose home was at Bethsaida in Galilee, and put their request to him. 'Sir, we want to meet Jesus.' Philip went and told Andrew: and together they came and told Jesus. And Jesus answered them – 'Now has the hour come for the Son of Man to be glorified. Truly I tell you, unless a grain of corn falls into the ground and dies, it remains just a solitary grain. But if it dies it brings forth much fruit. The man who loves his life (hoards it, keeps it safe) loses it. The man who hates his life (is ready to risk it and let it go) will find that he has kept it unto life eternal.'

Dying to live. Life – the life which is eternal – only at the price of dying. That is the truth which Jesus himself saw and vindicated. It is the truth of all effective Christian life, for the Church as for the individual. So long as our separated Communions are all 'loving their life', seeking to ensure that, whoever else may have to make sacrifices, lose something of their tradition and identity, *we* stay as we are, there can be no resurrection into the 'eternal life' of a reunited Church. That can only be won through readiness to die. And from that law none of us can plead exemption.*

* I have recently come across a striking confirmation of this principle in a very different context. Speaking of the suggestion that scientists should combine in resolutions in favour of world peace, Professor Heisenberg writes: 'Such resolutions may seem a welcome proof of good will. But anyone who speaks in favour of peace without stating precisely the conditions of this peace must at once be suspected of speaking only about the kind of peace in which he and his group thrive best – which of course would be completely worthless. Any honest declaration for peace must be an enumeration of the sacrifices one is prepared to make for its presentation.' *Physics and Philosophy* (Allen & Unwin, 1959), p. 165.

CHAPTER 12

Life in the Spirit

'THIRDLY I learn to believe in the Holy Ghost, who sancti-
fieth me and all the elect people of God.' So runs the familiar
definition of faith in the Church Catechism. It is likely
enough that the words awaken in many no great response
either of understanding or enthusiasm. We do not feel very
much at home with words like 'sanctification', 'saintliness',
'holiness'. There is a touch of remoteness, almost of pro-
fessionalism about them. We may even feel that they indicate
just that kind of character which we do not find attractive or
compelling: the kind which, in an immortal phrase of von
Hügel's, tends to occupy itself with 'little churchinesses'.
That, we feel, is not what a world sorely beset with moral
perplexity and spiritual emptiness really needs. What is more
it does not seem to reflect very faithfully the quality of life
which we see and reverence in the Gospels.

And yet we know in our bones that it is just here that our
real need lies. As we look back on the three preceding chapters, and acknowledge the urgency of the demands which
they make upon the Church, the need to make Christian
faith come alive in our contemporary world of thought, to get
to grips with the injustices and inequalities of our social and
international order, to break out of the stranglehold of division, we find ourselves at a standstill. Why are we so unable,
and unwilling, to face the demands? That is the real question.
And as we reflect on our powerlessness, some of the great
words of the New Testament echo in our hearts, 'life', 'fire',
'wind', 'power', 'love'. And we recognize in all of them the
reference to one common experience which those who use
them are trying to express, the experience of God realized in

action in the soul and in the community, present, insistent, quickening, renewing, inspiring, empowering – the Spirit.

Dimly and confusedly perhaps, we know that is what 'sanctification', 'holiness' really mean. And we know that there will be no effective revival of vitality in the Church, no breaking out into new ventures, no penitence which shames us into unity, unless they come through the influx of a transforming power which takes our rather tepid conventional 'Churchmanship' and turns it into what it is meant to be, 'Christlikeness'.

There is a passage in the Introductory Essay to a volume of Bishop Paget's sermons which brings out, as no words of mine could, the primacy of the Christian character.

There is one signal service which the appeal of the Christian character is peculiarly apt to render in the cause of faith. It is often the only power which can confront the steady, surreptitious, miserable pressure with which the sins of Christians fight against the cause of Christ. It may be that the contrast between these two forces covers by far the greater part of the whole battle-field; and that while critics and apologists with their latest weapons (or with the latest improvements of their old ones) are charging and clashing amid clouds of dust – with the world still thinking that there is the real crisis – the practical question between belief and disbelief is actually being settled for the vast majority of men by the silent and protracted conflict between the consistent and inconsistent lives of those who call themselves Christians. ... In many lives faith must have to hold on somehow through an almost overwhelming weight of discouragement in the hourly experience of the ill-temper, or injustice, or worldliness, or self-indulgence of religious people – it may even be of some who are actively ministering in God's name. And the one standby and stronghold through that dismal onset of unreality may be the known reality of the Christian character, the personal conviction that there are some at least on whom the grace of God is not bestowed in vain, in whom it does achieve its distinctive and transcendent work – the mind of Christ.*

* Paget (Longmans, 1902), pp. xxiv ff.

We shall have to turn back to the New Testament and look again at some of the things which these men say about the one fact of which, above all others, they are certain, the power of the Spirit of Christ to take the raw material of their nature and reshape it in his likeness.

Here are a few of them: 'The love of God is poured out into our hearts through the Spirit which he has given us' (Rom. 5:5). 'You are no longer living on the old level of "natural" life (in the flesh). You are living in the Spirit, since the Spirit of God has now come into your life' (Rom. 8:8, 9). 'The Spirit itself endorses the certainty in our own spirit, that we are indeed children of God' (Rom. 8:16). 'Don't you know that you are God's temple, in which his Holy Spirit dwells?' (1 Cor. 3:16). 'Because you are now God's sons, God has sent the Spirit of his Son into your hearts' (Gal. 4:6).

We may find some of the language difficult. We may not feel very sure whether what these men say has happened to them has happened to us. But some things at least are clear. That feeling of a remote God in a far-off heaven has gone. He is present in our own hearts. It is not a question, as Dr Vidler reminded us, of *praying for* the Spirit, of trying to summon him from a distance. It is a question of *living in* the Spirit, of recognizing his inspiration already at work in us, and of drawing upon it. (It is worth remembering that *pneuma* means wind, air. You can't live without breathing.)

How do they know this? By the surest possible evidence, the evidence of what he is doing with their own nature. 'The fruit of the spirit' (what grows in men's characters when the Spirit is at work) 'is love, joy, peace, patience, goodness, generosity, trustworthiness, unassertiveness, self-control' (Gal. 5:22). Of course we may not think that qualities such as these are particularly desirable. They haven't much cash value in the ordinary world; they don't necessarily lead to promotion and wealth. If we take that view of life, if what we really value are the qualities that seem to guarantee success, then it is not likely that we shall have much experience of this power of the Spirit to produce his distinctive fruit.

How does this fruit grow? As all fruit grows, by processes which man, for all his botanical and agricultural skills, does not wholly control. But at the same time, as those skills attest, there is much that man can do in preparing for and fostering growth. And in the spiritual life the same is true.

There is the practice of prayer. I shall never forget a remark which I once heard Oliver Quick make: 'I sometimes think that I know how to pray, until I read one of those devotional manuals, and then I discover that I don't.' Some of the rest of us share his experience. God knows that prayer is difficult enough: but the central idea of it is surely simple. It is the means by which we continually reaffirm, discern more clearly, and are strengthened for the following of, the true purpose of our life, that 'Christ may be formed in us'; that all our thinking and choosing and acting may be increasingly informed, shaped, directed by his Spirit. Everything is included in that: adoration, the thankful acceptance of that constant inspiration; penitence for the fact that we so constantly fall short of and betray it; petition, that in every situation in which we find ourselves we may try to be true to it; and intercession, that the grace which we seek for ourselves may be available for others, our personal friends, our Church, those who order the work of the world, those who direct the dealings of nations with one another.

What is true of prayer is true also of worship, which is the *corporate* acknowledgement by the people of God of this same purpose which governs all their common activities, the constant rededication to that purpose, the attempt to bring all the affairs of daily life under its control.

But prayer and worship, while indeed they are offered to God for his sole glory, are not, rightly regarded, ends in themselves. The power of the Spirit will never be fully experienced within the limited sphere of the sanctuary. In his lecture on the Holy Spirit in *Christian Belief* Dr Vidler has this passage:

A great book, a bell-ringing book, about the Holy Spirit could be written, though it might be in the form of a poem or a novel rather than a theological treatise. The reason why this book has not yet been written is that conscious experience of the presence and life of the Spirit among contemporary Christians is so thin and weak and hampered that conditions do not exist in which anyone can write with full-blooded conviction on the subject. It will not be written by any individual out of his own researches or mystical experience – not in the seclusion of a study or a cell – but by a member of a community which is making the discovery of what it means to live and act and change the world in the power and freedom of the Spirit.*

What he is pointing to of course is the truth implied in the title which I have chosen for this book. The Spirit is God *in Action*. And the experience of that comes as a by-product of, or rather as the direct response to, action: to the undertaking of some work in the cause of Christ on which we only embark with reluctance and even fear, because we know that it will be costly and demanding, and realize that as we stand we do not possess the knowledge or the courage or the staying power to tackle it.

The reason why much of our religious life, individual and corporate, is below par, conventional, and ineffective is just that we are not setting ourselves, or being called on, to cope with tasks of this demandingness. In our own lives we meet with situations of personal relationship in which we know that the only chance of effectively dealing with them lies in a supernatural response. I use the word in its literal sense. What is called for is just precisely an output of courage, patience, sensitiveness, forgiveness which, by nature, we feel is beyond us. 'I could never rise to those heights.' 'That is more than you can expect of human nature.' That is the kind of thing

* *Christian Belief* (S.C.M., 1950), p. 56.

we say. That is the way we let ourselves off. And just because of that we do not experience the influx of power. But on the occasions when we burn our boats, the miracle happens. '*Si crucem portas, portabit te.*' We find not that we are carrying the load, but that we and the load are being carried.

What is true at the individual level is equally true in the life of the Christian community or group. The experience of the Church overseas proves this every day. Kikuyu Christians, faced with the challenge of Mau Mau, or with the even more formidable task of salvaging and rehabilitating its victims; the agents of Inter-Church Aid, seeking to find the means of meeting the demand of yet one more situation of desperate need; an isolated Church, cut off from all contact with the Christian world by political restriction, these know the power which comes in response to obedience and courage. Our situations here at home are seldom as obvious or as dramatic. But they are there; and if we were more perceptive of what obedience to Christ's will really demands of us, we should see them more readily than we often do. Race prejudice and antagonism in back streets; encroachment on human liberty by ill-judged or even unscrupulous state action; the denial of fair dealing and honesty in an industrial demand or dispute; these are situations in which Christians ought to be ready to speak and act. How often we excuse ourselves on the ground that we don't see that there is anything that *we* can do about it. Could anything expose more clearly the extent to which our sense of proportion is astray? *We!*

When one studies the evidence of the New Testament and of Christian biography, there are, it would seem, certain dispositions which are essential to the experience of the power of God's Spirit. It was Bishop Gore who remarked that Christians should live 'with a permanent sense of dissatisfaction'. And no one who was privileged to know that great man could fail to understand what he meant by the phrase. There is the constant recognition that of all our work, of the whole quality of our life, the only thing that can honestly be said is: 'It could have been better.' That job, that personal interview, that sermon, that lesson in school – well, we did try to put our best into it; we did say our prayers about it; we did exercise some degree of responsibility or patience or courage. But 'it could have been better'.

Needless to say this is not an attitude which is in any way the monopoly of religion. It can be found as noticeably in the artist or the scholar or the craftsman or the research student. Underlying it there is the recognition and acknowledgement of an unattainable ideal, a beauty or precision which will be for ever beyond us. But if that is the attitude characteristic of any man whose heart and mind are set on the perfection of his work, how much more should it be true of those whose aim it is in some measure to have the mind of Christ. What possible ground for satisfaction or complacency can there ever be in any attempt of ours to reflect that strength and delicacy and precision? 'Brethren, I don't reckon that I have attained ...' No indeed!

By itself such a disposition could perhaps appear somewhat negative, discouraging, even a little morbid. But for the Christian it never should stand by itself. Accompanying it there is always the thankful recognition that to such humility there comes a response, indeed that the humility itself is evidence of an inspiration at work in us which prompts the dissatisfaction. And therefore the second disposition which opens the door for the Spirit's action is that of expectancy. Here indeed we touch the point at which the most character-istic note of the Spirit is to be discerned. If one recalls the three types of experience by reflection on which the doctrine of the Trinity was formulated, it is in the experience of the Spirit that the distinctively *forward-looking* emphasis is to be found, the leading on into new discovery of truth, the bringing out of new meaning and relevance in the things which belong to Jesus. 'It could have been better' may indeed be merely an acceptance of the imperfection of all human aspiration and effort, unless it is accompanied by the immediate inference – 'and there can be a better'. There is always the possibility of some fresh insight into, some fresh expression of, the mind of Christ. Every new situation with which we are confronted, whether in our individual lives or in the life of the Church, presents the chance of a discovery, a new act of creative thinking or living. The terrible blight of inertia, the lack of imagination, the refusal to believe that 'God has yet more light to break out from his Word', and more power to make that light operative if we will respond, are just the denial of the reality of the Spirit, and the surest way of stultifying his action in us.

I know well enough that there may be some among those who will read this book, as there will certainly be many among those who won't, to whom the religious language of the preceding pages will mean little or nothing. And not a few of them will be people of real spiritual sensitivity. Like Mr Corbett, they are conscious of the need of a truth which speaks to some of their deepest instincts and insights. But they do not find that truth in the traditional presentation of Christian theology or devotion. The very word 'God' is a 'dead' word; the virtue has gone out of the image; it no longer stands to them for a reality to which they can attach a meaning, still less for a being with whom they feel that a personal relation is possible.

And yet at the same time they are living at a spiritual depth at which they cannot rest content with the satisfactions which are afforded even by the pursuit of knowledge, or by dedication to the furthering of social justice and the meeting of human need, let alone the trivialities of much of their everyday existence. They are, perhaps dimly, aware in themselves of what 'Depth Psychology' would call the 'Deep Centre'. They have shared, even if only intermittently, that most profound of all human experiences which the story of the

Prodigal Son describes in the words 'When he came to himself'. That indeed is precisely what has happened. They discover their true selves. Beneath the medley of moods, contradictions, conflicting desires, which make up our day-to-day personality, they find a solid core of true self-hood which is the clue to the true character and direction of their lives.

It can, I believe, be claimed that this is precisely the point at which the Christian affirmation of the reality and activity of the Spirit comes into play. What that faith claims is that it is possible at this level of depth for the human spirit to be in contact with that which is the source of its very being, 'Lord and Life-maker'. Indeed that faith goes further and affirms that this sense of unsatisfiedness, this instinctive demand for an ultimate response, is itself the expression of the divine Spirit at work within man's soul.

The Spirit itself endorses the instinctive conviction of our own spirit that we have the life of God within us. ... We know that the entire creation is in a state of universal stress and anguish. And more than that, we ourselves, who have an instalment of the Spirit, we too share this inner distress, because we are still anxiously waiting for our true status of sonship. ... Thus the Spirit comes to the rescue of our powerlessness. We don't know what to pray for rightly (perhaps whether we can rightly pray): but the Spirit undertakes this for us with longings which can find no vent in words' (Rom. 8:16, 22 ff.).

It may well still seem to some that the clue here suggested is uncertain, that this link between the Spirit and our spirit (the crux of course of the whole business) is tenuous indeed. But, failing any other, it is worth following up the clue and seeing where it may lead us.

The ways in which it can be done are many. For some it will be possible to find and join a company of people whose worship is of a quality which leaves us in no doubt of its reality. We may not know what is the object of their worship. But the character of their lives makes it certain that it is not an illusion.

Others will not be able to go this length. But they may well be able to embark with some, like-minded with themselves, on an exploration of what the great spiritual masters of mankind have said about what they have found in their search.

Or it may be that they will take the line of practical action. There are more than enough causes and needs crying aloud for the work of men and women who will give themselves to something which will demand the utmost they can give.

One thing must be noted. In all these cases it is a *corporate* venture which is suggested. Whitehead in a much quoted phrase spoke of religion as 'what man does with his solitariness'. If he had said 'what man does to get away from his solitariness' he would have been much nearer the truth. For 'Life in the Spirit' is not an individual experience; it is the sharing in that fellowship which the Holy Spirit alone creates.

EPILOGUE

THERE was a moment when I contemplated giving this book the title 'Safety Last'. Wiser, or more cautious, counsels prevailed. But it will probably have been sufficiently clear that that has been the dominant note throughout. The work is indeed a plea for a more adventurous trust in the Spirit in the life both of the Church and of the individual Christian.

This accounts for what has been, and what has not been, said in it. I am well aware that there are other aspects of Christian life in which the Spirit is just as truly the inspiring and directing force. One has only, for instance, to reflect on the daily round of a parish priest and those who cooperate with him in the maintenance work of regular worship, visiting, and pastoral care. Much of it is routine, uneventful, unspectacular, but emphatically *not* undemanding. And those who give themselves to it are only sustained by continually drawing upon the resources of patience, devotion, sympathy, endurance, courage which are most surely the gift of the Spirit. The grace of God is bestowed, as we know on good authority, through a variety of personal channels to equip Christians for the work of serving; and the object of that service is the building up of the body of Christ, the slow patient shaping of the raw material of human nature into the pattern of a Christian community. Unless that essential spade-work is being done, there will be no Christian task-forces which can be called upon for special ventures.

But that is not, I believe, the whole story, and particularly so at the present time. In some parts of the world the Christian Church is patently fighting for its life. And even in the situations in which the conflict is not so obvious, the forces at work undermining the foundations of Christian faith and Christian moral standards are far more powerful and insidious than many of us like to acknowledge.

Nothing but an intelligent and well-planned strategy of counter-attack, and a tough and disciplined spirit to carry it through, will be adequate to meet the demand. There is a famous phrase which Cromwell coined to describe the kind of men that he looked for as captains of his Ironsides, 'Men who know what they fight for, and love what they know'. The Church could do with some more Ironsides.

BIBLIOGRAPHICAL NOTE

SWETE, *The Holy Spirit in the New Testament* (Macmillan, 1909), is still the best source-book for the New Testament evidence.

BARRETT, *The Holy Spirit and the Gospel Tradition* (S.P.C.K., 1947), is a work of exact scholarship which seeks to establish, on the basis of the evidence in the Gospels, the function of the Spirit in the teaching and ministry of Jesus.

KELLY, *Early Christian Creeds* (Longmans, 1950), is the most recent survey of the formative period of Christian doctrinal thought in the first five centuries.

QUICK, *Doctrines of the Creed* (Nisbet, 1938), is a well-known text book for the study of doctrine.

HODGSON, *The Doctrine of the Trinity* (Nisbet, 1943), and RAWLINSON, *Essays on the Trinity and the Incarnation* (Longmans, O.P.), contain valuable material.

STREETER (ed.), *The Spirit* (Macmillan, 1919), is one of the comparatively few books which attempts to relate the doctrine of the Spirit to the wider issues of Christian psychology and experience.

JENKINS, *Tradition and the Spirit* (Faber, 1951), and FISON, *The Blessing of the Holy Spirit* (Longmans, 1950), expound the Biblical doctrine of the Spirit in terms of its historical development in the Catholic and Protestant traditions of Church life.

VIDLER, *Christian Belief* (S.C.M., 1950), WHALE, *Christian Doctrine* (C.U.P., 1941), and MAURICE, *Theological Essays* (Clarke, 1956), contain valuable chapters on the Spirit.

More general books which contain illustrative material are NEWBIGIN, *The Reunion of the Church* (S.C.M., 1948) and *The Household of God* (S.C.M., 1953).

WILLIAMS, *The Descent of the Dove* (Faber, 1950), KNOX, *Enthusiasm* (O.U.P., 1950), and BERDYAEV, *Freedom and the Spirit* (Bles, 1935), stand by themselves as highly individualistic and illuminating studies of the Spirit in Christian history.

SCHWEITZER, E., *Spirit of God* (Adam and Charles Black), is an essential study of New Testament terminology and meanings.

Some more Pelicans
are described on the
following pages

The Pelican History of the Church

THE CHURCH AND THE AGE OF REASON
(1648–1789)

G. R. Cragg

A 505

This span in the history of the Christian church stretches from the age of religious and civil strife which existed before the middle of the seventeenth century, to the age of industrialism and republicanism which followed the French Revolution and the beginning of the Napoleonic wars.

The church in general, reacting strongly against the turbulences of the Civil War and the Thirty Years War, placed a premium on order, moderation, and stability. Movements suspected of enthusiasm, such as Puritanism, Quietism, and Jansenism, fell into disrepute, and the authority exercised by the state in religious affairs became more pronounced. It was an age dominated by Reason, which, until it provoked a reaction in such movements as Pietism and Evangelicism, posed a formidable challenge to Christianity.

In art and architecture, baroque gave way to rococo and then to neo-classicism, while church music was enriched by men like Vivaldi, Bach, and Handel.

CHRISTIAN FAITH TO-DAY

Stephen Neill

A 337

This book has developed out of lectures and mission addresses given by the author in a number of universities in the British Isles, in Canada, and in the United States, and out of the discussions following upon them. It has therefore grown directly from questions asked by students of the present day, and the perplexities felt by modern man as he tries honestly to come to terms with the Christian faith. No attempt is made to conceal what the Christian faith is, and what demands it makes; but equally no attempt is made to impose upon the reader by authority anything which he does not himself see to be true. Many lines of investigation are followed, and all are seen to converge towards a central point; by the last chapter it is evident that this central point is the ancient question, 'What think ye of Christ?'; and to the reader is left the responsibility of making an honest and serious response.

'This is a book for everybody. The sceptic will find in it a solid and formidable chain of reasoning; the inquirer will find himself firmly led from point to point; and the instructed Christian, even the skilled theologian, will encounter a great many profound considerations which he had not, or had only very vaguely, figured for himself' – *Church Times*